MW00587107

JESUS CRUCIFIED

The Baroque Spirituality of St Dimitri of Rostov

ST VLADIMIR'S SEMINARY PRESS
Treasures of Orthodox Spirituality Series
Number 1

The Treasures of Orthodox Spirituality Series provides translations of Orthodox spiritual literature from a variety of languages and periods. The series makes available a wide range of spiritual writings—prayers and hymns, meditations, homilies, hagiographies, letters, and autobiographical writings—that display how Orthodox Christians from various local traditions have followed Jesus Christ throughout the centuries. These translations are presented in an accessible yet scholarly format, with thorough introductions and notes that take current scholarship into account. As such, these readable and accurate translations will be of use to students, scholars, pastors, and lay Christians.

Series Editor
JOHN MIKITISH

Jesus
Crucified

THE BAROQUE SPIRITUALITY OF
ST DIMITRI OF ROSTOV

Text, Translation, and Introduction by

JOHN MIKITISH

ST VLADIMIR'S SEMINARY PRESS
YONKERS, NEW YORK
2017

Library of Congress Cataloging-in-Publication Data

Names: Dimitriĭ, Saint, Metropolitan of Rostov, 1651–1709, author. | Mikitish, John,
  translator.
Title: Jesus crucified : the baroque spirituality of St Dimitri of Rostov / by St Dimitri
  of Rostov ; translated by John Mikitish.
Other titles: Baroque spirituality of St Dimitri of Rostov
Description: Yonkers, NY : St Vladimir's Seminary Press, 2017. | Series: Treasures of
  Orthodox Spirituality series ; no. 1 | In English; translated from Russian.
Identifiers: LCCN 2017008669 (print) | LCCN 2017010734 (ebook) | ISBN
  9780881415780 (print) | ISBN 9780881415797 (electronic) | ISBN 9780881415797
Subjects: LCSH: Spiritual life—Orthodox Eastern Church. | Orthodox Eastern
  Church.
Classification: LCC BX382 .D565 2017 (print) | LCC BX382 (ebook) | DDC
  230/.19—dc23
LC record available at https://lccn.loc.gov/2017008669

COPYRIGHT © 2017 BY
ST VLADIMIR'S SEMINARY PRESS
575 Scarsdale Road, Yonkers, NY 10707
1-800-204-2665
www.svspress.com

ISBN 978-0-88141-578-0 (print)
ISBN 978-0-88141-579-7 (electronic)

All Rights Reserved

PRINTED IN THE UNITED STATES OF AMERICA

Жене

Theodore Jurewicz, *Saint Dmitry, Metropolitan of Rostov*,
iconographic wall painting on canvas, 2016. Holy Transfiguration
Orthodox Church, New Haven, CT. Photograph Irene Vassos.
Reproduced with permission.

A lamp to my feet is the law of the Lord, and his testimonies are a light to my steps, but I, crawling and knocked about in the darkness of ignorance, do not wish to obtain this lamp with the wise. But do you, O Dimitri, bright in appearance, come forward as a bridal escort, so that even I may hasten in spirit to wake early unto God out of the night.

—Canon to St Dimitri, tone 6, ode 5, troparion 1[1]

Let us bless Dimitri, the star of Russia, shining forth from Kiev and reaching unto Rostov through Novgorod of the north, brightening this whole land through teachings and wonders, the teacher of golden words. Indeed he wrote for the instruction of all, so that he, like Paul, might win all for Christ, and save our souls through right belief.

—Kontakion to St Dimitri, tone 8

Establishing the boundaries of the nations in accordance with the number of your angels and gathering all the scattered sons of Adam into your Church, therein do you multiply your saints, O our God, like stars in the sky, wherefrom shines forth also the memory of your holy hierarch Dimitri. For his sake enlighten our souls, darkened by discord of false belief, so that together we may cry out to you the fervent song: alleluia.

—Exapostilarion of St Dimitri

---

[1] All three hymns translated by the present author.

Table of Contents

Table of Abbreviations

BLDR = *Biblioteka literatury drevnej Rusi*

HUS = *Harvard Ukrainian Studies*

MGU = *Moskovskij gosudarstvennyj universitet*

PSTGU = *Pravoslavnyj Svjato-Tikhonovskij gumanitarnyj universitet*

RPTs = *Russkaja Pravoslavnaja Tserkov'*

STM = *St Tikhon's Monastery*

TODRL = *Trudy otdela drevnerusskoj literatury instituta russkoj literatury (Pushkinskogo Doma)*

Acknowledgments

First, I would like to thank Fr John Behr. His support and advice throughout the planning and completion of this project have been invaluable. My debt of gratitude to him is much larger than this, however. During my three years at St Vladimir's Seminary, he taught me how to read the fathers, not only in terms of external methodology, but in terms of an internal methodology: Fr John modelled real devotion, really hard work, real self-sacrifice in following Jesus Christ through encounter with him in the literary remains of his saints. So I am honored to have an opportunity to warmly thank Fr John for all of this and more.

Warm thanks are also due to Fr Ignatius Green, for a lot of work and a lot of good will on his part—and especially for many good catches of references that I missed or failed to note—and also to the rest of the staff at St Vladimir's Seminary Press, especially the Editor-in-Chief, Fr Benedict Churchill.

Fr Herman (Majkzrak) was a major source of enthusiasm and encouragement at this project's earliest stages. I am sure it would not have happened without his early support.

Particular and fervent thanks must go also to Paul Bushkovitch, Reuben Post Halleck Professor of History at Yale University, who urged me to look closely at the printed sources that serve as the basis for this translation and prompted me to revisit the work of I. A. Shljapkin much more carefully. Though I hit the same brick wall at the end, I was able to do so with much more confidence and verve.

These acknowledgements would be gravely incomplete without mention of two more names, those of Harvey Goldblatt, Chair of the Slavic Department at Yale University, and of Fr Michael Westerberg, rector of Holy Transfiguration Orthodox Church in New Haven, CT. The former is forever my father in Slavic philology, and the latter in the Orthodox Christian faith. Anything good in my work is really their good work, and the good work of all those I have named and forgotten to name, and all its defects—which are very many—are my own.

Finally, I, like many a translator before me, must end my acknowledgements with thanks to my wife, Matushka Brenda, who endured many nights of me staying up to 3 a.m. in the living room of our apartment, listening to Joni Mitchell's *Court and Spark* and translating, and who offered invaluable thoughts, or at least a listening ear, when I needed help with some of the most difficult passages.

Lord Jesus Christ, Son of God, through the prayers of St Dimitri, have mercy on us all!

Fr John Mikitish
New Haven, CT
30 August 2016
Venerable Alexander of Svir
Translation of the Relics of Right-Believing Prince Alexander Nevsky
Finding of the Relics of Right-Believing Prince Daniel of Moscow

Introduction

Life

St Dimitri of Rostov, known already in his own lifetime as the "Russian Chrysostom,"[1] was born in the village of Makarov, near Kiev, in December 1651,[2] to an apparently pious Cossack family.[3] Three of

[1] Ieromonakh Ioann (Kologrivov), *Ocherki po istorii russkoj svjatosti* [Essays on the History of Russian Sanctity] (Brussels: Zhizn' s Bogom, 1961), 274. Long before St Dimitri's time, St Cyril of Turov was honored with this title. See I. P. Eremin, "Literaturnoe nasledie Kirilla Turovskogo [The Literary Legacy of Cyril of Turov]," TODRL 11 (1955): 342.

[2] The exact date of his birth is unknown, but December 11 has been suggested. See M. A. Fedotova, A. A. Turilov, Ja. E. Zelinina "Dimitrij [Dimitri]," *Pravoslavaja Entsiklopedija* [Orthodox Encyclopedia], vol. 15 (Moscow: Izdatel'skij Sovet RPTs, 2007), 8. A. G. Mel'nik devotes a brief study to examining the day of the saint's birth and, more specifically, the day of his baptism. See A. G. Mel'nik, "Kogda byl kreshchen sv. Dimitrij Rostovskij [When Was St Dimitri of Rostov Baptized]?" in *Svjatitel' Dimitrij, mitropolit Rostovskij: issledovanija i materialy* [Holy Hierarch Dimitri, Metropolitan of Rostov: Studies and Materials] (Rostov: Spaso-Jakovlevskij Dimitriev Monastyr', 2008), 183–86.

[3] The summary here presented is based primarily on the accessible presentation given in Kologrivov, *Ocherki* [Essays], 266–85. For the most thorough investigation of St Dimitri's life, see I. A. Shljapkin, *Svjatoj Dimitrij Rostovskij i ego vremja* [Saint Dimitri of Rostov and His Era] (St Petersburg: Tipografija i khromolitografiya A. Transhel, 1891). For his official hagiography, see "Zhitie izhe vo Svjatykh ottsa nashego, Dimitrija, Mitropolita Rostovskago, Chudotvortsa [The Life of Our Father among the Saints, Dimitri the Wonderworker, Metropolitan of Rostov]," in St Dimitri of Rostov, *Sochinenija* [Works], vol. 1 (Moscow: Sinodal'naja Tipografija, 1839), 1–45. For an assessment of the hagiographical sources, see M. A. Fedotova, "Zhitie svjatogo Dimitrija Rostovskogo (k voprosu ob istorii sozdanija teksta) [The Life of Saint Dimitri of Rostov (Toward the Question of the History of the Creation of the Text)]," TODRL 60 (2009): 150–82. See also the summary of his life and works in Fedotova et al., "Dimitrij [Dimitri]," *Pravoslavaja Entsiklopedija* [Orthodox Encyclopedia], vol. 15, 8–30. Finally, for the most fundamental chronology, see especially St Dimitri's own diary, printed as the first appendix (*prilozhenie*) to Shljapkin, *Sv. Dimitrij* [St Dimitri], 3ff. (Note that Shljapkin's appendices are numbered separately from the main text, but also with Arabic numerals.)

St Dimitri's sisters entered the monastery, and Dimitri himself, after completing his education in Kiev, received the monastic tonsure at the age of 17 at Kirillov Monastery in the same city. He was ordained a deacon the following year, and after six years he was made a priest and a preacher of the diocese of Kiev.

At this point, an unsettled period in the saint's life began. In 1677, he went to Lithuania on pilgrimage, where he ended up remaining for another two years as a preacher attached to the Brotherhoood of the Transfiguration. After this, commanded by his Kievan superiors to return to Ukraine, he took up residence at the Monastery of St Nicholas in Baturin. Again after two years, he was appointed abbot of Maksakov Monastery in the region of Chernigov. Then, after less than a year, he returned to St Nicholas in Baturin, this time as abbot. Finally, in April 1684, he retired from his administrative duties for "unclear reasons." However, Kologrivov speculates that St Dimitri might have known ahead of time that, starting from the next month, May 1684, he would be called upon to undertake the compilation and composition of his magnum opus, the *Great Reading Menaion,* known in English as *The Great Collection of the Lives of the Saints,* or simply, in Slavonic or English, as *The Lives of the Saints.*[4] After just short of two years of uninterrupted work on this project, which saw the completion of the first volume (comprising the months of September, October, and November), St Dimitri was commanded to once again take up the duties of abbot at St Nicholas Monastery.

Upon the publication of this first volume in 1689, St Dimitri's work incurred the disapproval of the patriarch, Joachim, who accused him of teaching heresy: the Immaculate Conception of the Theotokos, for one, and the orthodoxy and sanctity of St Jerome, for another. In Kologrivov's depiction of events, an upset Dimitri was gathering materials to defend himself against Joachim's accusations and uphold his views when a trip to Moscow, in the company of Hetman Mazepa, led to an unexpected resolution: St Dimitri's gift of a copy of the first volume of the *Lives of the Saints* made a favorable

4Kologrivov, *Ocherki* [Essays], 269.

impression on Tsar Peter, and his difficulties with the patriarch were resolved without any retraction on St Dimitri's part.[5]

In 1692, St Dimitri managed to retire once more in order to devote himself to work on his *Lives*, but, from 1694, was obliged to serve as abbot of Glukhov Monastery. In the meantime, in 1693, the second volume of *Lives*, for the months of December, January, and February, was published. From 1697, he headed Kirillov Monastery, in Kiev, where he had begun his monastic life, and from 1699, he, newly raised to the rank of archimandrite, became the abbot of Elets Monastery in Chernigov. The third volume of *Lives* was published in 1700.

Finally, in 1701–2, having spent his last twenty-six years living at no less than five different monasteries—including multiple stints at three of those, having served as abbot at all five and retired from the abbacy three times—St Dimitri was at last raised to the episcopate and sent to Rostov, where he would spend the rest of his life. This did not happen without a hitch, however: St Dimitri was initially raised, by Peter's command, to the dignity of Metropolitan of Tobolsk and Siberia, succeeding Ignatius (Rimsky-Korsakov). But the saint's poor health, which delayed his departure from Moscow, brought a personal visit and leniency from the tsar, who sent him instead to the southern Russian city of Rostov. (Tobolsk and Siberia received another saint, Philotheus [Leshchinskij].)[6]

Upon his arrival in Rostov on March 1, 1702, St Dimitri visited, first of all, the church of the Conception of the Theotokos by St Anne at Savior-St George Monastery, where he set aside a place for his burial.[7] He then set about an ethusiastic program of educating

[5]Peter gave the saint a gift of "two luxuriant fox furs" in return. Ibid., 270–71.

[6]A work penned by St Philotheus, entitled *Lestvichnik* [Climacus], was found in St Dimitri's library upon the latter's death. It was apparently a gift from one saint to the other. See the fifth appendix to Shljapkin, *Sv. Dimitrij* [St Dimitri], 58. This work was recently re-discovered and published for the first time (under the title *Sibirskij Lestvichnik* [Siberian Climacus]) in 2015. The published version includes both a facsimile of the manuscript and a Russian translation. See Philotheus (Leshchinskij), *Sibirskij Lestvichnik* [Siberian Climacus] (Tyumen: Russkaja nedelja, 2015).

[7]Kologrivov offers the attractive speculation that the saint's choice of burial

a slothful, ignorant clergy and even more ignorant Christian popu-
lace. Long known as a preacher, in his position as metropolitan of
Rostov, the saint devoted himself not only to preaching, but also to
spreading his teachings by way of pamphlets. He worked "by word of
mouth and by letter"[8] to help amend the tremendous lack of knowledge and morality that afflicted his see. Particularly grievous was the
lack of knowledge of Scripture and the lack of understanding of, or
regard for, the mystery of the Eucharist. One of the saint's crowning
achievements, and greatest dissapointments, of this period was the
establishment of an academy in Rostov, on the model of that in Kiev,
which was shut down, in the saint's absence and without his prior
knowledge, for lack of funds after a mere two years.[9]

During his episcopacy, the saint's literary activity took a dis-
tinctly pastoral turn. It was in connection with his hierarchical
service that St Dimitri began his polemical engagement with Old
Belief, which resulted in his *Examination of the Schismatic Brynsk
Faith*, finished in 1709. (The final volume of *Lives* had appeared in
1705.) At the time of his death, the saint was working on a *Chronicle*,
intending it as a comprehensive introduction to scriptural history
and moral teaching for clergy ignorant of both.

Kologrivov paints this touching portrait of the saint during his
years of hierarchical service:

> Short of stature, blonde-haired, with streaks of grey, lean,
> stooped, with a pointed beard extending around his chin,
> wearing glasses, usually dressed in a dark green riassa (this was
> his favorite color), St Dimitri, on the exterior, did not give the
> impression of vigor. But this body, so frail, was ruled exclusively
> by a cheerful spirit, which spirit also called it to undertake no
> small exertion in labor, especially in spiritual labor. This labor

place was an affirmation of his belief in the doctrine of the Immaculate Conception.
Ibid., 273.

[8]Cf. 2 Thess 2.15.

[9]In his biography of the saint, Shljapkin devotes a whole chapter to this school.
Shljapkin, *Sv. Dimitrij* [St Dimitri], 321ff.

supported and strengthened it, so much so that, even at death's
doorstep, St Dimitri amazed those around him by the clarity
and firmness of his mind.[10]

By October 1709, exhausted by years of asceticism and pastoral
and literary labor, and, indeed, by the Rostov climate, the saint was
indeed at death's doorstep. I translate here in full the last entry in St
Dimitri's extensive surviving correspondence, his *Letter 40 to Theologus*, the latter a monk at the Monastery of the Miracle, in Moscow,
written on October 27, 1709, the day before his death:[11]

[27 October, 1709
Rostov]

Honorable sir, Theologus, my beloved!
    God save your charity,[12] for you fulfill all my desires and
requests. I have received the heretical catechesis,[13] looked at it,
and now I have sent it back to you. I saw it long ago, when I was
in Lithuania, only I completely forgot about its creators. I don't
have the time to be tied up with this:[14] would that God give
some other volunteer, but I am spent.
    You ask me, beloved, about my health, and I inform you
truly, I am infirm. Earlier my health was half and half: half
healthy, and half sick. But now sickness predominates, and now
hardly a third of my health remains, but I take courage in my
Lord and marvel [at him] in whose hands my life is. Now, I can't
do anything: before I manage to grasp it, everything falls from
my hands. My days have grown dark, my eyes see little; at night
a candle's light is not much help, but in fact makes it worse when
I look at writing for a long time; and my sickness obliges me to

[10]Kologriov, *Ocherki* [Essays], 277. The translation is that of the present author.
[11]Original text in M. A. Fedotova, *Epistoljar'noe nasledie Dimitrija Rostovskogo*
[The Epistolary Legacy of Dimitri of Rostov] (Moscow: Indrik, 2005), 122.
[12]Or, simply, "love."
[13]Fedotova states that this is a reference to the Protestant catechesis of Simon
Budny. Fedotova, *Epistoljar'noe nasledie* [Epistolary Legacy], 306.
[14]Literally, "harnessed to this."

lie down until I slumber. In this, my unhealthy [state of] health, I do not know what to expect, life or death. In this may the Lord's will be done. I am not ready for death, but, according to the will and command of the Lord, I should be ready. But my Master is powerful enough to strengthen my infirmity yet. This autumn has been hard on me; the Rostov air is very bad, and the waters are not healthy at all.

Forgive, beloved, I can write no more, and so I bow to you.[15]

Sinner Dimitri

St Dimitri died on October 28.[16] That evening, he summoned the cathedral's choir, and they sang to him three "psalms" of his own composition (translated in this volume; see pp. 119–23, below): "My Jesus most Beloved," "My hope I place in God," and "You are my God, Jesus." After sending the rest away, he thanked one in particular, who had been a great help to him in his literary endeavours, and told him a bit about his life of prayer as a child and youth. He added: "And you, children, should also pray." He sent the singer home with a prostration and with a single word, "*Blagodarju*," that is, "Thank you." The next morning, the saint was found dead, on his knees on the floor. St Dimitri had died at prayer sometime during the night.

Works

As a writer, St Dimitri is, together with his countrymen, co-workers, and friends Stefan Yavorsky and Feofan Prokopovich, the primary literary representative of the so-called Ukrainian (or "Cossack") Baroque. His *Lives of the Saints,* generally regarded as his most

[15]Literally, "I beat my forehead." This expression, "to beat one's forehead," *chelom biti,* is a commonplace in Old Russian letter-writing and there is a whole genre of petitionary letters, called *chelobitnye,* which is named for it. See Horace W. Dewey and Ann Marie Kleimola, "The Petition (*čelobitnaja*) as an Old Russian Literary Genre," *The Slavic and East European Journal* 14, no. 3 (Autumn 1970): 284–301.

[16]The entire paragraph following is based closely on the account in Kologrivov, *Ocherki* [Essays], 284–85. See also Shljapkin, *Sv. Dimitrij* [St Dimitri], 455–56.

important work, was originally published between 1689 and 1705. More than half of this collection is now translated into English, albeit with at least one notable omission, of St Dimitri's homily for the feast of the Conception of the Theotokos by St Anne, presumably for doctrinal reasons.[17]

Other major works published during his lifetime and immediately after his death include two works devoted to the miracles of the Mother of God and his *Examination of the Brynsk Faith*,[18] a refutation of teaching he ascribes to certain priestless Old Believers living in the Brynsk woodlands. At the time of his death, he was working on his *Chronicle*, a combination of sacred chronology and moral teaching aimed at combatting a grave ignorance of Scripture even and especially among the clergy. In addition to these major works, various pastoral letters, and also homilies, circulated among his flock, with his blessing, during his lifetime. After his death and canonization, though, many more works, including homilies, collections of spiritual and moral teachings, and dramatic works (including dramas for the Nativity of Christ and the Dormition of the Theotokos) were published, right up into the early years of the twentieth century. Among these posthumously published works are the devotional works translated here.

[17]St Dimitri of Rostov, *The Great Collection of the Lives of the Saints*, trans. Thomas Marretta, 8 vols. (so far) (House Springs, MO: Chrysostom Press, 1994–). In the December volume, under December 9, St Dimitri's homily for the feast of the Conception of the Theotokos by St Anne is replaced by a short and bland notice from the later Russian edition of the *Lives*. St Dimitri of Rostov, *The Great Collection of the Lives of the Saints*, trans. Thomas Marretta, vol. 4 (December) (House Springs, MO: Chrysostom Press, 2000), 171, esp. the translator's footnote. See also and notably the entry for the Nativity of the Theotokos in the September volume. St Dimitri of Rostov, *The Great of Collection of the Lives of the Saints*, trans. Thomas Marretta, vol. 1 (September) (House Springs, MO: Chrysostom Press, 2000), 152 and 155, esp. the translator's footnotes 6 and 18.

[18]Concerning the ambiguities surrounding the place of this work, and the struggle against Old Belief, as part of St Dimitri's legacy, see N. V. Ponyrko, "Dimitrij Rostovskij kak avtor Rozyska o raskol'nicheskoj brynskoj vere [Dimitri of Rostov as the Author of the *Examination of the Schismatic Brynsk Faith*]," TODRL 62 (2014): 34–42. Even the saint's ardent admirer, Kologrivov, assesses the work cautiously. See Kologrivov, *Ocherki*, 281.

Finally, it is important to note the number of devotional works that are, so far as I know and can tell, entirely spurious, which circulate under the name of St Dimitri to this day. These include the common devotion called *Prayers, Five in Number* (also called *The Tale of the Five Prayers*) and *The Psalter of the Mother of God*, based on *The Psalter of Mary*, a medieval Western work falsely attributed to Bonaventure.

Reception and Significance

Both as a writer and a "religious personality," St Dimitri has been generally well-received. In the words of literary scholar Prince D. S. Mirsky:

> Dimitri of Rostóv [*sic*] is a particularly attractive character. A great scholar and lover of books and learning, he was a peace-loving, meek, and charitable prelate who won the boundless love and gratitude of his flock. [...] He is the most exquisite fruit of the cultural revival of seventeenth-century Kiev.[19]

Mirsky adds, "He is particularly interesting as a playwright," and considers his dramas, together with those of Feofan Prokopovich, to be "serious works of genuine literary value."[20]

Approaching St Dimitri from a rather different point of view is the Russian convert to Roman Catholicism and Jesuit priest, the Hieromonk John Kologrivov, who considers the saint "one of the most attractive personalities in the history of Russian spirituality."[21] This appraisal matches that of a fellow Jesuit who met the saint in the flesh and called him "a man most excellent, a man (how rare!) of authentic sincerity."[22] As noted above, a good many of the saint's contemporaries, including churchmen such as Yavorsky and Pro-

[19]D. S. Mirsky, *A History of Russian Literature from Its Beginnings to 1900*, ed. Francis J. Whitfield (Evanston, IL: Northwestern University Press, 1999), 33.

[20]Ibid., 33 and 37.

[21]Kologrivov, *Ocherki*, 297. Trans. present author.

[22]Qtd. in ibid., 277. Trans. present author.

kopovich, and also Emperor Peter I himself, held him in similarly
high regard.

This high regard for St Dimitri has not been completely univer-
sal. Though Georges Florovsky concedes that the saint "in his spiritual life . . . was not confined to the narrow mold of a Latin world,"
he nonetheless claims that "as a thinker and writer [St Dimitri] was
never able to free himself from the mental habits and forms of theological pseudo-Classicism acquired when at school in Kiev . . . insist-
ing with obstinacy on their sacred character. . . . And in the north, in
Russia, where he settled, he never came to understand its distinctive
religious ethos and the circumstances that shaped it."[23]

Florovsky's appraisal of the Ukrainian Baroque and the Kievan
Academy, of their supposed initiation of a "pseudomorphosis" of
Orthodox thought, and of St Dimitri himself, has remained influen-
tial, and not just among the Orthodox, though it is especially among
Orthodox thinkers and writers that this perspective has flourished
and, in some circles at least, is taken for granted.

Offering a more balanced assessment is Metropolitan Hilarion
(Alfeyev), who considers St Dimitri an example of Orthodoxy without Byzantinism, and who situates the saint within his historical and
cultural context and points out parallels even with other saints who
did not share that context, such as St Nicodemus the Hagiorite.[24]

Despite the reservations of some—and it must be remembered
that suspicion of St Dimitri's "Latinizing" tendencies goes back to his
own lifetime—it is remarkable that, on the popular and institutional
level, St Dimitri has been received by the Russian and Ukrainian
Orthodox clergy and faithful without reservation.[25] Services for

[23]Georges Florovsky, *Ways of Russian Theology, Part One* (Belmont, MA: Nord-
land Publishing Company), 82.

[24]Metropolitan Hilarion (Alfeyev), "The Patristic Heritage and Modernity."
Paper presented at the 9th International Conference on Russian Monasticism and
Spirituality, Bose Monastery, Italy, 20 September 2001. Trans. Hildo Bos. http://ortho-
doxeurope.org/page/11/1/2.aspx.

[25]And not only Russian and Ukrainian: the 20th century Serbian bishop and
spiritual writer, St Nikolai (Velimirović) of Zhicha, includes St Dimitri in his own
version of the *Lives of the Saints*, *The Prologue of Ohrid*, assessing him in the following

both of his feast days are included in the standard *Menaion*. The saint was one of only five canonized by the Russian Church between the suppression of the office of patriarch and the reign of St Emperor Nicholas II, and, from the nineteenth century, he, together with Sts Tikhon and Metrophanes of Voronezh,[26] was known as one of the "Three Hierarchs of Russia," parallel to Sts John Chrysostom, Basil the Great, and Gregory the Theologian, the Three Hierarchs of antiquity.[27] At least two akathist hymns were composed in honor of the saint, and the second, officially approved by the censor, was printed no less than 18 times between 1799 and 1899.[28] His complete works appeared in several editions before the Revolution, and individual works or parts of works were printed many times. Today these works

way: "Dimitri was a great light of the Russian Church and of Orthodoxy in general. ... St. [sic] Dimitri of Rostov was a saint in the ancient and true model of the early Fathers." See St Nikolai Velimirović, *The Prologue of Ohrid*, trans. T. Timothy Tepsić, ed. Janko Trbović et al., 2nd ed., vol. 2 (Alhambra, CA: Sebastian Press, 2008), 456–7. Additionally, my friend, Fr Ignatius Green, has informed me that at least one prayer attributed to St Dimitri can be found in a Greek-language prayer book.

[26]The fourth and fifth saints canonized during this period were Ss Theodosius of Tot'ma, a monastic, and the missionary hierarch Innocent of Irkutsk.

[27]In answer to the Three Hierarchs' feast on January 29, the Three Newly-Revealed Hierarchs of Russia are celebrated on July 19. The feast is included in the standard *Menaion*, though only two hymns, a troparion and kontakion, are provided for its celebration. *Mineja ijul'* [July Menaion] (Moscow: Izdatel'skij Sovet RPTs, 2003), 407–8. To give a sense of the spirit of the celebration, I here provide a translation of the kontakion, in tone 3: "You who in our latter generations and later times comforted the sorrows of the souls of those bestormed by the stirrings of the passions of life, and those ill from the cold of faithlessness, warming [*sogrevavshii*] them with the warmth [*teplotoju*] of your faith, three newly-revealed hierarchs of Russia, Dimitri, Metrophanes, and Tikhon: make us firm on the rock of Orthodoxy and, as fathers who love your children, lead your spiritual children after you into the kingdom of Christ, by the steps of the fathers' commandments."

[28]A. B. Popov, *Pravoslavnye russkie akafisty* [Orthodox Russian Akathists] (Moscow: Izdatel'stvo Moskovskoj Patriarkhii RPTs, 2013), 95ff. and 533. It is notable that this second akathist to St Dimitri was one of the first ten or so ever officially approved for printing by the Synod. For more concerning the first (manuscript) akathist in honor of the saint, composed by the Priest Demetrius Mikhajlov in thanksgiving for a miraculous healing, see M. A. Fedotova, " 'Skazanie, koego radi viny izlozhisja Akafist svjatitelja Khristovu Dimitriju' (ob odnom chude svjatogo Dimitrija Rostovskogo) [*A Narration Concerning the Reason for Which This Akathist Was Set Forth* (Concerning One Wonder of Saint Dimitri of Rostov)]," TODRL 62 (2014): 120–42.

can be found online with ease, in any number of versions, which
are often edited to make them less obscure for the modern reader.
Excerpts from these works were used as the dogmatics "textbook"
of St Petersburg Academy precisely when the Orthodoxy of the
school's curriculum needed to be ensured.[29] Perhaps even more
telling, St Dimitri's name is used to this day to legitimize various
devotions, such as the *Five Prayers* and *The Psalter of the Mother of
God*.[30] Finally, as one may infer from my footnotes, Russian language
scholarship on St Dimitri is fairly voluminous.

Selection of Works

Now something must be said about the selection of works translated here. All of them, with the exception of the letter translated in
Appendix I, are "devotional," by which I mean prayers, or prayerful
meditations, for private use.[31]

First in the collection are two similar works, *Greeting the Members, or Wounds, of Our Lord Jesus Christ Every Day* and *A Prayer, or,
A Brief Recollection of Christ's Sufferings*. The latter of these seems to
be an expansion and re-working of the former. Both prayers "greet"
each of the suffering members of Christ in the same order, with those
members in parentheses inserted in this order in the second work
only: head, face, eyes, (nose), lips and throat, ears, neck, (shoulders),
hands and arms, breast, (heart), (inner parts), side, knees, feet, body,
blood, soul. The first work then concludes this list with a general
"greeting": "Rejoice, joy of all." Both works end with a prayer, though
these are dissimilar in length and content.

[29]Florovsky, *Ways*, 256.

[30]This (mis)use of St Dimitri's name is a long-standing practice. The akathist
hymns in honor of the Protection of the Theotokos and the Passion of the Lord were
both misattributed to St Dimitri in the eighteenth and nineteenth century. See Popov,
Akafisty [Akathists], 135–45. Indeed, even concerning some of the works translated in
the present volume, see the several cautions scattered throughout this Introduction.

[31]Concerning the possibility that either the *Verses on the Lord's Passion*, or *The
Council and Judgment of the Unbelieving Jews against Jesus of Nazareth, the Redeemer
of the World*, or both, are in fact dramatic works, see below.

Next come two devotions for communion. The first of these, the *Worship of the Most Pure Mysteries of Christ*, is clearly intended for the use of a priest or bishop, for insertion into the usual communion rites of the liturgy. This is apparent in any number of ways, but perhaps the most obvious is that the work assumes that the communicant will receive the body and blood separately, a form of communion reserved, in Eastern Orthodox practice, for the major clergy alone. The second of these, *Discerning Divine Communion*, is a preparatory meditation for participation in the Eucharist.[32]

Then come three works of "worship" (*poklonenie*), addressed to the Theotokos, the Trinity, and Christ, all of which follow a similar structure: an introduction based on the hymn *Come, Let us Worship*;[33] a main body, consisting of a number of prayers beginning "I worship" (*poklonjajusja*); and a concluding prayer based on the hymn *It Is Truly Meet*.[34] The acts of "worship" in the main body are addressed both to the persons themselves as well as events (the Annunciation or the Nativity). In *Worship of Jesus Christ*, a good portion of the main body is once again devoted to Christ's wounded members. This section is similar to *Greeting the Members* and *A Brief Recollection*, but the ordering of the body parts is quite different, and, notably, each of the five wounds is "worshipped" separately.

The next two selections, "Prayers for Deliverance from Blasphemous Thoughts" and "A Very Brief Method for Defeating Blasphemous Thoughts," are in fact excerpted from the larger work *Spiritual Therapy for Confusion of Thoughts, Collected in a Brief Form from Various Patristic Books*. Though the second of these is not a devotional work strictly speaking, being neither a prayer nor a

[32]These two works, with a third work of a catechical or didactic character (actually placed first in order), are all put together under a single heading (*Concerning Communion of the Holy Mysteries*) in the print edition. I am not at all sure these three works (or parts of works) belong together, and the character of the third work (or part of a work) is not in keeping with the contents of the present volume. As such, I translate these two works (or parts of works) as if they were indeed separate compositions. See St Dimitri of Rostov, *Sochinenija* [Works], vol. 1, 262–74.

[33]See below, p. 57, footnote 1.

[34]See below, p. 59, footnote 12, and also p. 63, footnote 17.

meditation, it does contain very concrete instructions for a practice of prayer, and so is included here.

Next are three lengthy meditations on the Passion: *A Godly Contemplative Meditation on the Most Holy Sufferings of Our Lord Jesus Christ*; *A Thankful Recollection of the Sufferings of Christ and a Prayerful Meditation, More Useful than All Other Prayers, Which Should be Performed on All Fridays*; and the *Lamentation for the Burial of Christ*. The *Godly Contemplative Meditation* is an ordered collection of meditations on various events of the Passion and each meditation is followed with a recitation of the Lord's Prayer and a bow. This work ends with a contemplation of the seven words of the Savior on the cross.[35] The *Thankful Recollection* takes on a para-liturgical structure, with a beginning typical for public or private prayer, followed by thirty-three "recollections" (one for each year of Jesus' earthly life).[36] The *Lamentation*, on the other hand, has no explicit cues for prayer, bows, or the like, and only the final three verses of the meditative poem end with supplication. In the first two of these meditations especially, St Dimitri often expands on the scriptural accounts, providing many additional, and often violent, details for contemplation.

With these three long Passion devotions, and following them, I translate *The Council and Judgment of the Unbelieving Jews against Jesus of Nazareth, the Redeemer of the World*, the least obviously "devotional" of all the works in this collection. Its form is that of a play, of sorts, in which various Jews (most wholly invented, with unusual names) give opinions about what should be the fate of Jesus.[37] Some, including Joseph of Arimathea and Nicodemus,

[35]Though the table of contents of the nineteenth century edition on which this translation is based lists this latter contemplation as a separate work, it is printed as part of the *Godly Contemplative Meditation*, of which it is manifestly a part. See St Dimitri of Rostov, *Sochinenija* [Works], vol. 1, ii.

[36]Once again, though the table of contents of the nineteenth century print edition lists the catalogue of ecclesiastical historians and teachers about the Passion as a separate work, it is manifestly a part of the *Thankful Recollection*. See ibid.

[37]Shljapkin prints a slightly different, slightly expanded version of this text from a manuscript version in his eighth appendix to *Sv. Dimitrij* [St Dimitri], 72ff. See

attempt to defend Jesus, or demand an account of his crimes. Most, however, demand his punishment, be it by exile or crucifixion. The work ends with Pilate's declaration of Jesus' sentence.

Though this work may appear to be a drama on the surface, that it is a drama intended for performance seems unlikely: there are many characters, and each speaks only once. Moreover, there is no apparent action or movement, and work is extremely short.[38] Granted, it could be a fragment of a lost or never completed drama; however, more likely, it is simply intended as a private meditation, albeit in pseudo-dramatic form, on the judgment of Jesus. I therefore choose to translate it here alongside many other Passion-focused meditations and devotions.

Next are three devotional poems by the saint: *The Address of a Sinner to Magdalene, Weeping at the Feet of Christ*; the *Psalms, or, Spiritual Cantos*; and the *Verses on the Lord's Passion*. The first two of these works are straightfoward devotional poetry; the third, and longest, introduces eleven children, who "carry" and speak about the instruments of Christ's Passion. Most of poem is put in the mouth of these eleven characters.

The presence of these "children" raises the possibility that the *Verses* are in fact a dramatic work, St Dimitri's version of a Passion

especially his notice on p. 76. He notes that at least one other manuscript exists and that this manuscript ascribes the work to Simeon Polotskij, and Shljapkin describes the attribution to Dimitri as *mnimnoe*—alleged but false. Indeed, Shljapkin supposes that the work is a translation from an inscription accompanying some "foreign" print depicting the judgment of Jesus, which was translated into Slavonic when the accompanying iconography was adopted in Russia. However, the existence of "similar" inscriptions on wall paintings from the seventeenth or eighteenth century hardly proves that the work is itself a translation, subsequently copied from wall inscriptions into manuscripts, though that the work drew inspiration from such iconographic depictions (and accompanying inscriptions) seems certain (and see also below, p. 113, footnote 17). None of this serves as an argument for the work's attribution to St Dimitri; however, I include the work here in deference to the print editions. Even if the work does not belong to St Dimitri, it certainly says something about his place and his time.

[38]Granted, the version printed by Shljapkin divides the speakers into two groups, one on the left and one on the right, and mentions that Jesus sits in the midst of all, on a chair, hands bound, but there is still no movement. Ibid., 72–74.

play.[39] The other, certainly dramatic, works of the saint are largely allegorical, and avoid directly portraying Christ, his Mother, and so on.[40] The introduction of eleven children, the bearers of the intruments of the Passion, would have enabled St Dimitri to stage a drama on the crucifixion without portraying the event or its protagonist, that is, the Lord Jesus Christ, directly, and that the play calls for eleven "children" raises the distinct possibility that the work was intended for performance by the students of his Rostov school.[41] However, speeches—or in this case, songs—assigned to numbered children figure in at least one Polish poetic work from the latter part of the sixteenth century.[42] As such, the dramatic nature of the *Verses*

[39]E. V. Zhigulin, "Istochnikovedenie teatra Svjatitelja Dimitrija Rostovskogo [Studying the Sources of the Theatrical Works of Hierarch Dimitri of Rostov]," in *Istorija i kul'tura Rostovskoj zemli 1993* [History and Culture of the Land of Rostov 1993] (Rostov: Gosudarstvennyj muzej-zapovednik "Rostovskij kreml'," 1994), 139–45. This possibility was also suggested (though not necessarily endorsed) by Dushan Bednarsky in his article, "Blood and Tears, Love and Death: Seventeenth-Century Devotional Homoeroticism and Tuptalo's 'Verses on the Lord's Passion,'" *Canadian Slavonic Papers* 38 (1996): 71.

[40]See Dimitri of Rostov, "Komedija Rozhdestvo Khristovo [Comedy for the Nativity of Christ]," in BLDR 18 (St Petersburg: Nauka, 2014), 522–73, and Dimitri of Rostov, *Uspenskaja drama* [Dormition Drama], ed. M. N. Speranskij (Moscow: Tipografija Shtaba Moskovskogo voennogo okruga, 1907). Both plays feature angels, and the latter features the forefather Jacob (in conversation with angels and "the spirit of prophecy") and the apostle Thomas (in conversation with "doubt" and "hope"), but that is as far as they go.

[41]Note that Act 1, Scene 5 of St Dimitri's *Dormition Drama* features six numbered children lamenting the translation of the Theotokos to heaven. Concerning the dating of this work and the possibility that it may not have been written for St Dimitri's students in Rostov, see M. A. Fedotova, "O neizdannykh sochenijakh svjatitelja Dimitrija Rostovskogo: k postanovke problemy [On the Unpublished Works of Hierarch Dimitri of Rostov: Toward a Definition of the Problem]," *Vestnik* PSTGU III 37 (2014), 57.

[42]Jan Kochanowski, "St. John's Eve," trans. George Rapall Noyes, ed. Marjorie Beatrice Peacock, *Slavonic Review*, 6.17 (1927): 401–14. Selections from the same work are anthologized in a bilingual format in Michael J. Mikoś, *Polish Literature from the Middle Ages to the End of the Eighteenth Century: A Bilingual Anthology = Literatura polska od średniowiecza do konca XVIII w.: antologia w jezyku polskim i angielskim* (Warsaw: Constans, 1999), 276–83. Granted, in Kochanowski's poem, written, according to Noyes, some time between 1571 and 1584, the twelve girls' songs are part of the plot, as it were, and there are no indications of anything like movement, unlike in the *Verses*.

remains only a possibility, and not a strong one, though Fedotova
considers it one of his "declamations," the same as the Nativity and
Dormition dramas.[43] Moreover, even if this were a dramatic work,
the content of the *Verses*, focused on the instruments of the Passion,
has much in common with the saint's works undoubtedly intended
for private devotion, such that, whether *Verses* is intended for dramatic performance or private prayer, it has its place alongside the
other works in this collection.

The final three works in this collection are prayers: *General
Confession of Sins, Pronounced by a Penitent before a Priest*; *Prayer
of Daily Confession to God of a Person Laying Down a Beginning of
Repentance*; and an *Untitled Prayer*. Among all the works in this
collection, the first two of these prayers are perhaps those least obviously influenced by Western Christian spirituality.[44] The format, and
much of the content, of the *General Confession* is familiar from many
similar, and earlier, compositions, which circulated in the Orthodox
East, and the *Prayer of Daily Confession* is filled with Orthodox
liturgical commonplaces and phrases derived from many earlier
devotional prayers, these latter still in use for private morning and
evening prayer and private communion preparation.

The final prayer, given no title in the printed edition (apart from
its superscription, "The humble Dimitri, Metropolitan of Rostov
and Yaroslavl, wrote this for the use of his own wretchedness," and
the placeholder title, "By the same Dimitri, Metropolitan of Rostov,
for the particular use of his soul," given in the table of contents),[45] is
largely addressed to the reader himself, in the first person, though
it ends with an appeal to Christ and a few verses addressed to the
reader in the second person. This prayer in particular, with its strong
emphasis on the infamy of death, is reminiscent of earlier Slavic

[43]Fedotova, "O neizdannykh sochenijakh [On the Unpublished Works]," 56.

[44]A glaring exception to this is the opening of the *General Confession of Sins*,
which is clearly based, whether directly or indirectly, on some form of the *Confiteor*.
See below, p. 149, footnote 1. My thanks to Fr Ignatius Green for pointing this out
to me.

[45]St Dimitri of Rostov, *Sochinenija* [Works], vol. 1, ii.

para-liturgical works, especially the hymns of Stephen the Fool of Galich, penned in the second half of the seventeenth century,[46] though these in turn are undoubtedly influenced by the much older Orthodox funeral service.

The first appendix comprises a translation of St Dimitri's *Letter 22 to Theologus*. The letter, written on Bright Monday, 1708, is abundant in Paschal joy and offers a curious "allegorical" interpretation of the traditional red Easter egg. This letter shows the saint's exegetical skills in a different context, and its focus on the resurrection complements the focus on the cross throughout much of the remainder of the volume.

Last of all, the second appendix features a psalm written to St Dimitri, published with the *Psalms, or Spiritual Cantos*, in 1889, apparently the work of Archpriest Aristarchus Izrailev, the editor of that publication (see below). If nothing else, it is a testament to the continuing influence of St Dimitri's devotional works over one hundred years after his death.

A final word, this one concerning works not included in this collection: St Dimitri has been named, by some Ukrainian scholars at least, as the author of a considerable body of devotional poetry not included in nineteenth-century printed editions.[47] The existence of these works, or the possibility that they may belong to St Dimitri, has been largely ignored, to my knowledge, in Russian-language scholarship. The translation and analysis of these additional works is a matter for another book, or another several books.[48]

[46]For the text and commentary, see N. V. Ponyrko, "Stikhi pokojannye galitskogo jurodivogo XVII v. Stefana [Penitential Verses of the Seventeenth Century Fool-for-Christ Stephen of Galich]," TODRL 56 (2004): 596–600.

[47]See Bednarsky, "Blood and Tears, Love and Death," 73, and the works cited there, esp. the works attributed to St Dimitri included in *Ukrains'ka poezija, kinets' XVI — seredina XVII ct.* [Ukrainian Poetry, from the End of the Sixteenth Century to the Middle of the Seventeenth Century], vol. 2, ed. V. I. Krekoten', M. M. Sulima (Kiev: Naukova Dumka, 1992), 278–329 (see 607–15 for relevant notes). For the nineteenth century printed editions of St Dimitri's work, see the brief discussion immediately following this section.

[48]For a related issue—that of the continual discovery of previously unpublished works by the saint—see Fedotova, "O neizdannykh sochenijakh [On the Unpublished Works]," 50 *et passim*.

Texts and Authenticity

When St Dimitri died, in accordance with his wishes, the manuscripts and drafts of his works were buried with him.[49] Though
numerous manuscripts of the saint's works have survived, including
many "authorized" copies from the saint's own scriptorium, some
with marginalia, corrections, and so in the saint's own hand,[50] only
the published versions of most of his works were available to me,
and these are based haphazardly on whatever manuscripts could be
found;[51] furthermore, these printed editions may include certain
Synodal "corrections."[52] Accordingly, the vast majority of the translations in this collection of his devotional works are from nineteenth-

[49]Some of his letters exist in autograph copies, and the first volume of his *Lives of
the Saints* also survives in a pre-publication autograph. See this brief but illuminating
and thorough study: A. A. Kriming, "Podlinnye rukopisi svjatogo Dimitrija Rostovskogo v sobranijakh Rostova [Manuscripts Attributed to Saint Dimitri of Rostov in
the Collections of Rostov]," in *Istorija i kul'tura Rostovskoj zemli* [History and Culture
of the Land of Rostov] 1993 (Rostov: Gosudarstvennyj muzej-zapovednik "Rostovskij
kreml," 1994), 18–24. See also M. A. Fedotova, "O dvukh aftografakh Dimitrija
Rostovskogo [On Two Autographs of Dimitri of Rostov])," TODRL 50 (1996): 537–43,
and V. A. Esipova, "Dve rukopisi kruga Dimitrija Rostovskogo (Po materialam
nauchnoj biblioteki Tomskogo gosudarstvennago universiteta) [Two Manuscripts
from the Circle of Dimitri of Rostov (According to Materials from Tomsk National
University)]," TODRL 62 (2014): 614–27.

[50]Regarding "authorized" copies of the saint's works, see Fedotova, "O neizdannykh sochenijakh [On the Unpublished Works]," 50. Note further that some of the
works included here, such as the *Lamentation for the Burial of Christ*, definitely do
exist in authorized copies. See ibid., 56.

[51]I have been able to locate, but not view, manuscript copies of at least some of
the works translated in this collection. See the entries for mss 619/417, fols. 271 and
621/811, fols. 257 and 287 in T. N. Protas'eva, *Opisanie rukopisej Sinodal'nogo sobranija*
[Description of the Manuscripts of the Synodal Collection], pt. 1 (Moscow: Glavnoe
arkhivnoe upravlenie pri Sovete Ministrov SSSR / Arkheograficheskaja komissija pri
Akademii Nauk SSSR / Gosudarstvennyj istoricheskij muzej, 1970), 37 and 40. (I am not
positive whether the first work cited here, from ms 619/417, *O pochitanii svjatykh tain*
[Concerning the Honoring of the Holy Mysteries], corresponds with *Discerning Divine
Communion, Worship of the Most Pure Mysteries of Christ*, both, or neither; see also p. 26,
footnote 32, above.) The first edition of the collected works of St Dimitri, printed in 1786
in 6 volumes, was based on a four volume collection of St Dimitri manuscripts owned
by Ja. A. Tatishchev, who also funded this initial printing. See Fedotova et al., "Dimitrij
[Dimitri]," *Pravoslavnaja Entsiklopedija* [Orthodox Encyclopedia], vol. 15, 13.

[52]See Kologrivov, *Ocherki* [Essays], 271.

century print editions of St Dimitri's collected works, specifically, the five-volume edition of 1839–49.[53] Exceptional are the *Psalms, or, Spiritual Cantos,* published in 1889, together with a "psalm" to St Dimitri himself (see Appendix II),[54] and the *Verses on the Lord's Passion.*[55]

This latter work deserves a special note. Bishop Amphilochius of Uglich published it in 1889, together with the facsimile of the manuscript on which it was based, which he believed to be in St

[53]St Dimitri of Rostov, *Sochinenija* [Works], 5 vols. (Moscow: Sinodal'naja Tipografija, 1835–49). Vol. 5 was published in 1835, vol. 1 was published in 1839, vols. 2 and 3 were published in 1840, and vol. 4 in 1849. For a basic bibliography of some of the various editions, see Fedotova et al., "Dimitrij [Dimitri]," *Pravoslavnaja Entsiklopedija* [Orthodox Encyclopedia], vol. 15, 13. I note that this particular five volume edition appears to remain a standard reference for scholars. See, for example, A. O. Krylov's candidate dissertation: A. O. Krylov, *Mitropolit Dimitrij Rostovskij v tserkovnoj i kul'turnoj zhizni Rossii vtoroj poloviny XVII—nachala XVIII vv.* [Metropolitan Dimitri of Rostov in the Ecclesiastical and Cultural Life of Russia from the Second Half of the Seventeenth Century to the Beginning of the Eighteenth Century] (cand. diss., MGU, 2014), 45–46. Krylov lists the place of publication for the edition he used as St Petersburg; however, the page numbers and years of publication for each volume match those of the Moscow edition I use here.

[54]St Dimitri, *Psalmy, ili Dukhovnye Kanty* [Psalms, or Spiritual Cantos], ed. Aristarch Izrailev (Moscow: Tipografija L. i A. Snegirevykh, 1889). For a discussion of manuscript texts of these and other psalms, see E. E. Vasil'eva, "Pesennoe nasledie svjatitelja Dimitrija Rostovskogo [The Legacy of the Songs of St Dimitri of Rostov]," *Istorija i kul'tura Rostovskoj zemli 1993* [History and Culture of the Land of Rostov 1993] (Gosudarstvennyj muzej-zapovednik "Rostovskij kreml'," 1994), 18–24. Vasil'eva, who describes a manuscript containing eleven psalms, speculates in passing that the *Lamentation* and *Verses*, translated here, once formed a devotional unit—an early form or relative of the *Passija* service?—with some of the psalms from this collection, though I am not sure of her basis for this idea.

[55]As noted above (p. 31, footnote 48), individual works of St Dimitri, not included in the early collected works, were discovered and published throughout the nineteenth century and continue to be discovered published into the twenty-first century. For an example of this, see M. A. Fedotova, "O neizdannykh propovedjakh Dimitrija Rostovskogo: Slovo na perenesenie moshchej svjatogo muchenika Dimitrija tsarevicha [On the Unpublished Works of Dimitri of Rostov: A Homily on the Translation of the Relics of the Holy Martyr Dimitri the Tsarevich]," TODRL 63 (2014): 184–204. A complete edition of the saint's works—much less a critical edition thereof—remains a desideratum. See Fedotova, "O neizdannykh sochenijakh [On the Unpublished Works]," 50.

[56]In the introduction to his publication, Bishop Amphilochius provides the his-

Dimitri's own hand.[56] However, A. A. Kriming, in his study of authentic St Dimitri autographs, has concluded that the handwriting is definitely not that of the saint, and has called the attribution of the work into question, albeit tacitly.[57] With that said, I see no reason to question this work's authenticity more than any of the other works included here. Without compelling evidence against the attribution of the work, and without a more compelling alternative attribution, there is no substantial reason to consider the *Verses* anything but an authentic work of the saint, even if the manuscript reproduced by Amphilochius was not, indeed, in the saint's own hand.[58] I would note that St Dimitri's library contained a work, hand-written and apparently in Slavonic, entitled *The Passion of Christ* (*Strasti Khristovy*).[59] Could there be a connection with the work published by Bishop Amphilochius and translated here?

tory of the manuscript as he received it from its previous owner, Priest Peter Bazhenov. Amphilochius quotes the latter as follows: "Presenting to Your Grace, here attached, the *Passion Verses*, composed and written out by the hand of Holy Hierarch Dimitri of Rostov himself, I request, in a manner entirely humble, that Your Grace receive these verses into your holy foundation [that is, Holy Savior-St James Monastery] as a most precious deposit, in memory of Holy Hierarch Dimitri of Rostov, the Wonderworker, just as they were received by the rector of your foundation, the reposed Fr Archimandrite Innocent [Bp Amphilochius adds in a footnote that Innocent was rector in 1813, and died in 1847], from the maiden Daria Sergeevna Sokovnina, the daughter of His Excellency Sergius Petrovich Sokovnin, on September 21, 1830 [September 21 is the primary feast day of St Dimitri, established in 1757—*present author*]. These verses were found in the books of my reposed father-in-law, Fr Deacon Nicholas Vasil'evich Pisarevskij, of Porech', which came down to him as an inheritance from his uncle, Fr Archimandrite Innocent, who had been rector of Holy Savior-St James Monastery." His Grace Amphilochius adds: "On the first quarto, sewn into the notebook of the *Verses*, this is written by S. P. Sokovnin, in red ink: 'The *Passion Verses* composed by St Dimitri, Metropolitan of Rostov, and written by his own hand.'" See Amfilokhij, Predislovie [Foreword], in St Dimitri (Tuptalo), Metropolitan of Rostov, *Stikhi na Strasti Gospodni ili Stikhi Strastnye* [Verses on the Lord's Passion, or, Passion Verses] (Yaroslavl: Tipografija Gubernskago Pravlenija, 1889), i–ii.

[57]Kriming, "Podlinnye rukopisi [Manuscripts Attributed to St Dimitri]," 24.

[58]Fedotova, for her part, accepts the attribution of the work to St Dimitri. See above, p. 30.

[59]See the fifth appendix in Shljapkin, *Sv. Dimitrij* [St Dimitri], 58. The book's title is given in Slavonic (Latin titles are transliterated throughout the list) and it is described as a *pisanaja kniga*, that is, a "manuscript book."

Sources

St Dimitri's familiarity with a considerable number of Western devotional and dogmatic writers is well known. Not only must he have studied various Latin writers during his time as a student in Kiev, but his personal library was also stocked with the works of Western religious authors: Thomas Aquinas, Bonaventure, Cornelius a Lapide, Peter Canisius, Martin Becan, Thomas à Kempis, various works of Latin hagiography, and so on.[60] The influence of Roman Catholicism in particular (devotion to the five wounds and the heart of Jesus,[61]

[60]Kologrivov, *Ocherki* [Essays], 299, and Florovsky, *Ways*, 82. Florovsky concludes, "On the whole it was a library appropriate to an erudite Latin." Indeed, St Dimitri was engaged with Western European learning quite broadly. See for example his *Letters* 2 and 3 (themselves written in Latin) to Isaac Vanderburg, in which he either thanks Vanderburg for sending, or requests the sending of, the following Latin volumes: the *Bibliotheca Sacra* of Peter Ravanellus (a theologian of the Reformed tradition); the *Mellificium Theologicum* (the author is not named in the letter, but this is apparently a reference to the work of this name by Johannes Binchius); the New Testament (apparently in Latin); works by Mark Frederic Wendelin (a Protestant theologian); works by Francis Bacon; the *Ars Concionandi*, by William Price (a Puritan); *Loci Communes Sacrae Theologiae* (once again, the author is not named, but this is apparently a reference to the 1567 work of this name by the Protestant dogmatician Wolfgang Musculus); the works of Sulpicius Severus; *The Theater of History*, a world history by Wilhelm Stratemann; and works by Sethus Calvisius (a German scientist and composer) and Gabriel Bucelin (a Benedictine humanist). See the full texts of the letters in Fedotova, *Epistoljarnoe nasledie* [Epistolary Legacy], 172–75. For complete bibliographic information for the works in question, see her notes, 335–36. Finally, for St Dimitri's complete cell library, see the fifth appendix to Shljapkin, *Sv. Dimitrij* [St Dimitri], 54–58. For the heavily (or even almost exclusively) Latin and Polish libraries of some of St Dimitri's predecessors and contemporaries, see Ryszard Łuźny, "The Kiev Mohyla Academy in Relation to Polish Culture," HUS 8.1/2 (1984): 125–27.

[61]Kologrivov contends that it was unlikely that devotion to the Sacred Heart *per se*, in its fully-realized form—sprung up as it was only in 1673 to 1675, and in France to boot—influenced St Dimitri, but supposes rather that his devotional focus on Jesus' heart owed its impetus to similar Western sources such as that of Margaret Mary Alacoque. Kologrivov, *Ocherki* [Essays], 300. This is a subject for an essay rather than a footnote, but suffice it to say here that Kologrivov underestimates both the development and reach of the devotion to Jesus' heart even before Margaret Mary Alacoque began to communicate her visions to her Jesuit confessor, Claude de la Colombière. For a (relatively) widely available overview in English, see the discussion in Gerald B. Phelan's Introduction to John Eudes, *The Sacred Heart of Jesus*, trans. Richard Flower (New York: P. J. Kennedy & Sons, 1946), esp. xiii–xxv, and most esp. xxiff.,

devotion centered on the seven words spoken on the cross,[62] belief
in the Immaculate Conception, Western-style eucharistic piety) on

and note further that not only public celebration of the heart, initiated in France by
John Eudes, pre-dates the visions, but also that an early tract concerning devotion
to Jesus' heart, *Meta Cordium, Cor Iesu*, was the work of Gaspar Druzbicki, a Polish
Jesuit who died in 1662. (See Jean Bainvel, "Devotion to the Sacred Heart of Jesus," in
The Catholic Encyclopedia, vol. 7 [New York: Robert Appleton Company, 1910], 166.
Thanks to the library staff at Sacred Heart Seminary and School of Theology, I also
had access to a scan of the 1885 edition of this work while preparing this introduction:
Gaspar Druzbicki, *Meta Cordium, Cor Iesu*, ed. P.-X. P., new ed. [Angers: Typi Lachese
et Dolbeau, 1885].) In other words, even if St Dimitri did not know about Margaret
Mary Alacoque's version of this devotion, there is a possibility—though only a possibility—that he was familiar with earlier forms of devotion to Jesus' heart that were
very well developed on their own terms, even if they were to be later surpassed by and
considered mere antecedents to the type of devotion urged by Margaret Mary Alacoque. In this regard see also Raymond Jonas, *France and the Cult of the Sacred Heart:
An Epic Tale for Modern Times* (Berkeley and Los Angeles: University of California
Press, 2000), 14 and 95. Coming to my attention too late for me to consider it here
was Jon L. Seydl's unpublished disseration, containing useful introductory material
and a good discussion and bibliography of the traditional, "genealogical" presentation of the history of the devotion to the Sacred Heart. See Jon L. Seydl, "The Sacred
Heart of Jesus: Art and Religion in Eighteenth-Century Italy" (PhD diss., University
of Pennsylvania, 2003), 9ff.

[62]For Late Medieval Western devotion to the five wounds and the seven words,
see the discussion (albeit focused on distant England) in Eamon Duffy, *The Stripping
of the Altars*, 2nd ed. (New Haven: Yale University Press, 2005), 238–56. For an overview of the devotion to the five wounds from antiquity to the nineteenth century, see
Frederick G. Holweck, "The Five Sacred Wounds," in *The Catholic Encyclopedia*, vol. 15
(New York: Robert Appleton Company, 1912), 714–15. Likewise, devotion to the seven
words remained part of the Roman Catholic spiritual patrimony in the Early Modern
period and beyond. To give but two examples, Robert Bellarmine, during an annual
retreat, composed a work specially devoted to this subject, *De Septem Verbis Christi*,
published in 1618, and Alphonsus de Liguori, writing in the eighteenth century, after
the time of St Dimitri, includes several meditations on the seven words in his work
The Passion and Death of Jesus Christ. See Sydney Smith, "St. Robert Francis Romulus
Bellarmine," in *The Catholic Encyclopedia*, vol. 2 (New York: Robert Appleton Company, 1907), 413, and, in English translation, Alphonsus de Liguori, *The Passion and
Death of Jesus Christ*, trans. Eugene Grimm (New York: Benziger Brothers, 1886),
279–301 *et passim*. (This latter work, though of a somewhat later period, gives a very
good sense of the general type of Western devotional writing that probably inspired
many of the items translated in the present volume.) Finally, it is important to note
that the devotion to the five wounds and seven words was present in early modern
Poland in particular. See, e.g., the adaptation of these devotions in Gaspar Druzbicki,
Tractatus de variis Passionem Domini nostri Iesu Christi Meditandi modis ad fidelium

his works is obvious. Indeed, his *Worship of the Most Pure Myster-ies of Christ* begins with a paraphrase of the famous *Anima Christi* prayer.[63]

Despite the many confluences that have been noted among vari-ous streams of Latin spirituality and the various works of St Dimitri, much work remains to be done with respect to identifying more spe-cific influences,[64] especially on the works translated here.[65] Indeed, for my own part, I have in most instances failed to identify, even in a general way, the anonymous "doctors"—likely Latin church writers such as Bernard and Bonaventure (or their pseudonymous equiva-lents)—whom St Dimitri cites several times. That said, I would like to point out just one more likely influence, that of the forms of devotion that would become, well after St Dimitri's time, the familiar Stations of the Cross. The Stations of the Cross, nowadays ubiquitous in the Roman Catholic world, grew out of a re-creation of the Via Dolorosa in Jerusalem through chapels and stations, a devotion soon amplified, from at least the sixteenth century, by the publication of manuals for contemplating these "stations," sometimes numbering more than

Christi utilitatem conscriptus (Lublin: Georgius Forsterus, S. R. M. Bibliopola, 1652), 182ff. and 349ff.

[63]See below, p. 51.

[64]Of course, the search for, and identification of, influences—whether general or specific—does not imply that St Dimitri simply aped Latin (or other) devotional writings and the trends they may represent. But on what points, and to what degree, he drew inspiration from such writings is nevertheless a meaningful question, and one that cannot be answered until a detailed study of potential influences has been undertaken. This last is a task whose probable complexity is enormous, given that much of the possibly relevant Latin material is little studied.

[65]St Dimitri's devotional and poetic works of the type translated here have received comparatively little scholarly attention in comparison with his letters, homilies, and works of moral and spiritual advice. (Cf. Fedotova's recent study of the *Apologija vo utolenie pechali cheloveka, sushchago v bede, gonenii, i ozloblenii . . .* [Apology for Assuaging the Sorrow of a Man Who Is in the Midst of Affliction, Per-secution, and Malice . . .], which examines in detail the question of the influences on the work and which proves it to be an authentic work of St Dimitri: M. A. Fedotova, "'*Apologija vo utolenie pechali cheloveka, sushchago v bede, gonenii, i ozloblenii . . .*': k voprosu ob avtore teksta ['Apology for Assuaging the Sorrow of a Man Who Is in the Midst of Affliction, Persecution, and Malice . . .': Toward the Question of the Text's Author]," TODRL 64 [2016]: 121–39.)

38   ST DIMITRI OF ROSTOV

thirty.[66] Though she does not pursue the argument with systematic
vigor, Ju. N. Zvezdina suggests some parallels between the *Thankful
Recollection* and Central European artistic and architectural develop-
ments coming into vogue in East Slavic lands during the period.[67]
Given the particular popularity of "calvaries" (series of chapels
devoted to different events of the Passion) in Poland and Lithuania
during this era, more could be made of this argument.[68] In the meantime, I would merely suggest that at least three of St Dimitri's long
Passion meditations included here—the other two being the *Godly
Contemplative Meditation* and the *Lamentation for the Burial*—are
likely inspired by this Western devotional trend.

All this said, St Dimitri's familiarity with Latin works of piety and
theology is not so singular[69] and "Kievan" as some may assume.[70] For

[66]See the overview in G. C. Alston, "Way of the Cross," in *The Catholic Encyclopedia*, vol. 15 (New York: Robert Appleton Company, 1912), 569–71.

[67]See Ju. N. Zvezdina, " 'Blagodarstvennoe strastej Khristovykh vspominanie' sv.
Dimitrija Rostovskogo i otrazhenie temy v kul'ture XVII veka [*A Thankful Recollection of Christ's Passion*, by Saint Dimitri of Rostov, and the Reflection of (This) Theme
in the Culture of the Seventeenth Century])," in *Istorija i kul'tura Rostovskoj zemli 1996*
[History and Culture of the Land of Rostov 1996] (Gosudarstvennyj muzej-zapovednik "Rostovskij kreml'," 1997), 173–78.

[68]See Elżbieta Bilska-Wodecka, *Kalvarie Europejskie: Analiza struktury, typów, i
genezy* (Cracow: Institut geografii i gospodarki przestrzennej UJ, 2003), esp. 103–8,
and also her article, "Pielgrzymki do sanktuariów meki pańskiej w Polsce – geneza,
przemiany, współczesność," *Peregrinus Cracoviensis* 4 (1996): 233–42.

[69]Certainly many of his fellow graduates of the Kiev Academy were equally
fond of Latin sources. For example, St John (Maksimovich) of Tobolsk (a relative of
St John [Maksimovich] of Shanghai, so famous in our own day) published translations of both Protestant and Catholic devotional works. For the earlier St John and
his works, see V. V. Busygin et al., "Ioann (Maksimovich, Ivan) [John Maksimov-
ich]," in *Pravoslavnaja Entsiklopedija* [Orthodox Encyclopedia], vol. 23 (Moscow:
Izdatel'skij Sovet RPTs, 2008), 219–30. And St John and St Dimitri were not the only
Latin-trained scholars from Ukraine and the Polish-Lithuanian Commonwealth to
have successful careers in Russia. For the influential activities of the Kiev-educated
Epiphanius Slavinetskij; Simeon Polotskij, an Orthodox monk and scholar from what
we would now call Belarus; and others, see Paul Bushkovitch, *Religion and Society in
Russia: The Sixteenth and Seventeenth Centuries* (New York: Oxford University Press,
1992), 150–75 *et passim*.

[70]Cf. again the characterization of St Dimitri in Florovsky, *Ways*, 82, and, more
generally, 64–85 and 104ff.

example, collections of Marian miracles and related tales, such as *The Great Mirror*[71] and *The Star Most Bright*,[72] this latter a collection of miracles related to the Rosary in particular, were being translated into Slavonic in Russia well before the time of Peter, and one may wonder whether familiarity with such collections, whether in Latin or Slavonic, might have in some way influenced St Dimitri's early published collection of Marian miracles, *Dewy Fleece*. To give another example, some of the works of Peter Skarga, which exercised a considerable influence on St Dimitri's works, had been available in Slavonic since before the latter's time, and later in the eighteenth century, St Paisius of Hilandar, a Bulgarian active in a Serbian monastery on Mt Athos, was making extensive (and, of course, unacknowledged) use of Skarga's historical works in his own.[73] Considering the extent of Skarga's readership, it is worth underscoring the point made by Ryszard Łuźny: the Latin influence on the East Slavs during this period was of a specifically Polish character, and, insofar as it was mediated through Poland, was already "pre-Slavicized."[74]

[71]See the overview in E. K. Romodanovskaja, "'Velikoe Zertsalo' [The Great Mirror]," in *Pravoslavnaja Entsiklopedija* [Orthodox Encyclopedia], vol. 7 (Moscow: Izdatel'skij Sovet RPTs, 2004), 507–10.

[72]See the discussion of this work and the related icon, based on the Roman Catholic image of Our Lady of the Rosary, in E. P. R., "'Zvezda presvetlaja' [*The Star Most Bright*]," in *Pravoslavnaja Entsiklopedija* [Orthodox Encyclopedia], vol. 19 (Moscow: Izdatel'skij Sovet RPTs, 2008), 734–35 and L. P. Tarasenko, "'Zvezda presvetlaja' ikona Bozhiej Materi [The Icon of the Mother of God 'Star Most Bright']," in *Pravoslavnaja Entsiklopedija* [Orthodox Encyclopedia], vol. 19 (Moscow: Izdatel'skij Sovet RPTs, 2008), 736–37.

[73]Florovsky, *Ways*, 82. Ryszard Łuźny notes that Skarga's own version of the *Lives of the Saints*, consulted by St Dimitri a generation later, was already to be found in the library of Simeon Polotskij. See Łuźny, "The Kiev Mohyla Academy," 126. For the history of Skarga's version of Baronius in Slavic lands—it was known in Russia in Slavonic even during the Time of Troubles—see Harvey Goldblatt, "On the Language Beliefs of Ivan Vysens'kyj and the Counter-Reformation," HUS 15.1/2 (1991): 31, esp. note 99.

[74]"In the sixteenth and seventeenth centuries the Renaissance, the Reformation, and the Baroque came to much of this area in a modified Polish form, made more 'familiar' by being Slavic. When we speak about the so-called Polish impact on the culture of another nation, we must remember that this 'Polishness' was frequently reducible to the functions of an intermediary or transmitter of West European

In any case, St Dimitri's sources are not only Latin. Though Georges Florovsky declares that "Greek and Old Church Slavonic materials are hardly present at all" in St Dimitri's works, and that "there is" in them "scarcely a trace of the diction and idiom of the East,"[75] the devotional works translated here abound with the language of Orthodox worship, as I often highlight in my notes, and, at the end of the *Thankful Recollection*, St Dimitri even provides a list of sources, compassing ancient writers both Greek and Latin.[76] Additionally, St Dimitri quotes St John Chrysostom[77] at length in his work on the seven words spoken by Christ on the cross, appended to his *Godly Contemplative Meditation*,[78] and in his *Letter 22 to Theologus*, translated here in Appendix I, he asks his friend Theologus to buy a copy of Andrew of Caesarea's *Commentary on the Apocalypse* on his behalf and send it to him. Indeed, he specifically notes that, although he had access to Andrew via citations in Latin books, he would like to read Andrew himself in Slavonic. It is clear, then, that St Dimitri was not without knowledge of Orthodoxy's Greek heritage.[79] And with regard to St Dimitri's familiarity with Old Church Slavonic sources, one need look no farther than

influences over two centuries. Western values could penetrate eastward and be adapted and assimilated by national cultures there because they had already been tested and accepted on the banks of the Vistula, Bug, Neman, and Dniester." Łużny, "The Kiev Mohyla Academy," 124.

[75]Florovsky, *Ways*, 82.

[76]See below, p. 101. Granted, he may have had his primary access to some of the Greek fathers only in Latin translation.

[77]Or at least, St Dimitri quotes a homily attributed to St John Chrysostom. I was unable to find the source for the quotation.

[78]See below, pp. 88–89. Note also in this regard that St Dimitri included, in addition to his own homilies, a considerable number of Patristic homilies by or attributed to St John Chrysostom and St Basil the Great in his *Lives of the Saints*. Furthermore, his *Examination of the Brynsk Faith* begins with a citation from a homily attributed to Chrysostom, taken, in fact, from the *Margarit*, a famous Slavonic collection of homilies attributed to St John. See St Dimitri of Rostov, *Rozysk o brynskoj vere* [Examination of the Brynsk Faith](Moscow: Sinodal'naja Tipografija, 1855), iii.

[79]Even if he did not know Greek and knew the Greek Fathers primarily, if not exclusively, in Latin (and, to a lesser degree, Slavonic) translation. Cf. Esipova, "Dve rukopisi [Two Manuscripts]," 615.

his devotion to Ss Anthony and Theodosius of the Caves, to whom he wrote a canon, still in liturgical use to this day.[80] St Dimitri's library even contained a volume of the works of St Maximus the Greek (not yet canonized in the early eighteenth century), a favorite of the Old Believers who, despite his moniker, wrote most of his works in Slavonic.[81]

Conventions

I have sought to make this translation, first and foremost, as accurate and, therefore, as consistent as possible. In every possible case, the same word is translated in the same way. Needless to say, oversights are probable, and some words, in particular common verbs and especially prepositions, simply cannot support a single translation in all instances. Additionally, I could not avoid situations in which multiple words share a single translation. For example, I render both *shchedrota* and *blagoutrobie* as "compassion." When such words appear in quick succession, however, I try always to include a footnote to distinguish them.

In connection with this goal of accuracy and consistency, I chose not to render scriptural citations according to any English translation in particular, and sought instead to simply translate the Slavonic as St Dimitri gives it. This, I believe, offers a double benefit: the English vocabulary used is consistent between the scriptural citations and the rest of the translation, and the reader does not get the false

[80]See *Mineja sentjabr'* (Moscow: Izdatel'skij Sovet RPTs, 2003), 61–73. For the canon's original publication, see "Kanon Prepodobnym Antoniju i Feodosiju Pecherskim [Canon to Venerable Anthony and Theodosius of the Caves]," in *Khristianskoe chtenie* [Christian Reading] (June 1859): 427–35. The composition is rich in its use of scripture and sophisticated in its structure, using various and original refrains, which vary by ode (there is no obvious refrain for ode 5, and ode 9, though it repeats words and images at the end of each troparion, cannot be said to have a refrain either) and come at the end of each troparion. The theotokia are apparently also compositions of St Dimitri, and their refrains match those of the other troparia. St Dimitri also composed a (still unpublished) service to the Holy Nine Martyrs of Cyzicus. See Fedotova, "O neizdannykh sochenijakh [On the Unpublished Works]," 59–60.

[81]See the fifth appendix in Shljapkin, *Sv. Dimitrij* [St Dimitri], 57.

impression that St Dimitri made use of the RSV, NKJV, etc. When citing the Bible, I always cite the Psalter according to the Septuagintal numbering. Otherwise, I use the chapter and verse numbering usual in English-language Bibles, unless otherwise noted.

For the translation, in footnotes, of common liturgical hymns and prayers, I have often relied on no prior translation in particular; however, my familiarity with the translation of prayers most common in the Orthodox Church in America, exemplified in the *Divine Liturgy* book of 1967,[82] has ensured that, in most cases, the translation I provide is at the least close to this standard.

I hope that the result of all of my efforts in this regard, while imperfect, does allow a reasonable chance for the reader to analyze St Dimitri's use of certain terms and phrases without the need for constant correction of the translation against the original. With that said, no translation can ever replace recourse to the original, and the reader who does not yet know Slavonic is encouraged to learn it!

For the convenience of the non-specialist reader, all Russian and Slavonic words are transliterated here. In my transliteration, I use *j* for й, *y* for ы, and ' for ь. Hard signs (ъ) are ignored (the " sign seemed too cumbersome and unusual for the uninitiated reader). Both э and e are transliterated *e*. The Slavonic nasal vowels are rendered as they are pronounced in contemporary Russia, as *ja* and *u*.

First names are given in their standard English form, rather than transliterated, except in cases where the figure is especially likely to be familiar to English readers under his transliterated name (Feofan Prokopovich, for example, or Stefan Yavorsky—or, most importantly, St Dimitri himself). The first or last names of Russians well-known to English-speaking readers in a less-exacting transliteration than mine (for example: Dimitri, Florovsky, Mirsky, Yavorsky) are given in their well-known form (not as, for example: Dimitrij, Florovskij,

---

[82]For the most recent edition, see *Divine Liturgy* (South Canaan, PA: STM Press, 2013).

Mirskij, Javorskij). Finally, I use the Russian forms of names and places, rather than their Ukrainian forms, supposing that the former will be more familiar to most readers. In short, when it comes to transliteration, expedience trumps consistency.[83]

---

[82]A final note: in St Dimitri's meditations on the crucifixion, he often speaks about the "the Jews" in a way that some readers may find disconcerting—indeed, shocking—and perhaps offensive. Whatever contemporary people may think of it, we must realize that such rhetoric is not peculiar to the saint, but part of a tradition of Christian discourse running from the Gospel according to St John and through the services of the Orthodox Church to our saint and beyond. In such cases, "the Jews" in question are not the modern racial-ethnic or religious group(s) we may have in mind when we hear St Dimitri's words, but, first, those Jews who did, after all—according to the Gospel accounts—participate in the killing of Jesus Christ, and, second, and more importantly, a theological representation—the Jewish law in contrast to Christianity's grace (Jn 1.17), or human sin to divine mercy. This is why St Dimitri can ask any penitent to call himself a friend of Judas, a companion of the crucifiers, and—perhaps truly shockingly—a second devil (see p. 155, below). For more on how to understand this sensitive subject, see Met. Hilarion (Alfeyev), *Orthodox Christianity, Volume IV: The Worship Services of the Orthodox Church* (Yonkers, NY: St Vladimir's Seminary Press, 2016), 336–37, and especially footnote 42. Though I did not have time to reference it in preparing this note, I also recommend that the reader consult Alexander Pereswetoff-Morath, *A Grin without a Cat*, 2 vols. (Lund: Lund University Department of Slavonic Studies, 2002), for an assessment of the function of such rhetoric in medieval Russia in particular. (The situation in the time and place discussed by Pereswetoff-Morath was different, no doubt, from that in St Dimitri's early modern East Slavdom, but the former also undoubtedly forms an important part of the background to the latter.) Finally, I note that although St Dimitri speaks of the "deicide Jewish race" (see p. 95, below), we must acknowledge that his concepts of race and ethnicity were neither our twenty-first concepts nor those "scientific" concepts of race, born in the nineteenth and brought to their awful conclusion in the twentieth, that are so fundamental to many forms of anti-Semitism. He certainly knew about people-groups and bloodlines—the nations of Genesis 10—and that God does judge nations (see e.g. Ps 109.6 and Mt 25.32) and generations (see e.g. Mt 17.17; "generation" another possible translation of *rod*, which I translate "race," and it is in fact this same word, *rod*, that occurs in the Slavonic of Mt 17.17), but I think that it is safe to say that he did not have any concept of race like those we share (and contest), based as they are on a very particular and modern blend of social, cultural, historical, intellectual, and religious factors.

1

Greeting[1] the Members, or Wounds, of Our Lord Jesus Christ Every Day

Rejoice, most holy head of our Lord Jesus Christ, awesome to all dominions, for our sake crowned with thorns and beaten with a reed.

Rejoice, most exceedingly beautiful face of our Lord Jesus Christ, for our sake spat upon and struck.

Rejoice, most marvelously merciful eyes of our Savior Jesus Christ, for our sake moistened with tears.

Rejoice, lips and throat of our Lord Jesus Christ, for our sake given gall and vinegar to drink.

Rejoice, most exceedingly precious ears of our Lord Jesus Christ, for our sake filled with blasphemies and insults.

Rejoice, neck of Jesus Christ our Savior, adorned with humility, withered for our sake—and back, for our sake beaten and wounded.

[1]*Tselovanie* could also mean "kissing," but more usually means "greeting." (Of course, St Dimitri does mention the prayerful kissing (*lobyzanie*) of Jesus' wounds elsewhere: see below, p. 109.) In connection with this, it is important to note that "rejoice," which occurs so often here, is my translation of the Slavonic word *radujsja*, which occurs in Luke 1:28 and in many liturgical hymns (particularly in the *chaire-tismoi* of the Akathist, a hymn and genre of hymnography to which this and the following work have a definite similarity). Especially in the case of the Gospel text, many English translations render the Greek word as "hail." But since the Slavonic word is what one might call an etymological rather than contextual rendering of the Greek, I in turn translate the Slavonic *radujsja* as "rejoice" rather than "hail" or some other greeting. Much more could be said about this issue of "rejoice" versus "hail," but this footnote is not the place. For an example of where the translation "rejoice" is absolutely necessary, see below, p. 141.

Rejoice, most pure hands and arms of our Lord Jesus Christ,
    for our sake stretched out on the cross.
Rejoice, most pure breast of Jesus Christ, our Savior, for our
    sake filled with sorrow during the Passion.
Rejoice, most pure side of our Lord Jesus Christ, for our sake
    opened wide by a soldier's lance.
Rejoice, most pure knees of Jesus, for our sake bowed in prayer.
Rejoice, much-suffering, most pure feet of our Savior, for our
    sake nailed to the cross.
Rejoice, whole body of our Lord Jesus Christ, for our sake
    broken on the cross, and wounded, and afterward buried.
Rejoice, most precious blood, poured out from the body of the
    Lord Jesus, our Savior.
Rejoice, most holy soul of our Lord Jesus Christ, for our sake
    surrendered into the hands of the God and Father on the
    cross.[2]
Rejoice, joy of all. Amen.
O most pure and life-creating cross of the Lord! With the
    power of Christ, who was crucified upon you, make me
    mighty against all visible and invisible foes, guarding me
    from temptation of flesh and soul.

With bows.

[2]Cf. Lk 23.46.

2

A Prayer, or, A Brief Recollection of Christ's Sufferings

Rejoice,[1] head of our Lord Jesus Christ, before which all powers tremble, for our sake torn at the hair, crowned with thorns, beaten with a reed, and afflicted even unto the brain.

Rejoice, face of our Savior, most precious, more beautiful with comeliness than any of the sons of men,[2] shining with divine appearance, inciting desire in angels,[3] and marvelous for all [to behold], for our sake spat upon, covered with dishonor, slapped by hands, all bruised, having neither appearance nor comeliness.

Rejoice, eyes all-merciful, brighter than the sun, drawing the gaze of the hearts of all to yourself, [eyes] for our sake moistened with tears and streaming with blood.

Rejoice, nose most divine, which breathes the scent of spiritual fragrance and for our sake endured the stench of vomit from lawless, defiled, filthy lips.

Rejoice, mouth dripping with honey[4] and throat most sweet,[5] for our sake given gall and vinegar to drink.

Rejoice, ears all exceedingly honorable, which for our sake endured unutterable insult, blasphemy, and dishonor.

[1]See above, p. 45, footnote 1.
[2]Cf. Ps 44.3.
[3]Cf. perhaps 1 Pet 1.12.
[4]Cf. Song 4.11, though this phrase is applied to the "bride" in the biblical text.
[5]Cf. Song 5.16.

Rejoice, neck all-humble and guiltless of sin, for our sake
     withered and led unto the crucifixion by a rope.
Rejoice, shoulders most holy, for our sake lashed at the pillar
     by the violent scourges of executioners and all lacerated
     even unto the bones.
Rejoice, hands and arms all-powerful and almighty, for our
     sake tied in torment, and, when the cross was brought,
     nailed thereto.
Rejoice, breast[6] most meek, granting rest greater than
     Abraham's bosom[7] to your friends and companions,[8] for
     our sake agitated by the unbearable horror of passion and
     torment, and which endured beating by the executioner's
     whips together with the ribs and belly.
Rejoice, heart ever-living, which for our sake was wounded by
     deathly sorrows, sadness, and the lance.
Rejoice, all you most compassionate inner parts, which for
     our sake are tormented beyond measure by bitter pains
     surpassing nature.
Rejoice, side God-pouring [and] most glorious, for our sake
     pierced even unto the heart by the soldier's lance, and from
     which poured forth blood and water,[9] from which was
     established the font of the life-creating mysteries, seven in
     number, for our cleansing and sanctification.
Rejoice, knees honorable and all-worshipped, bent to the earth
     in prayer and falling to earth and rock under the cross.
Rejoice, feet honorable and all-worshipped, which for our sake
     were nailed to the cross together with the hands.
Rejoice, entire body of our Lord Jesus Christ, for our sake
     crucified on the cross between two thieves, wounded
     without mercy, having no part whole from head to feet,
     slain, and buried.

[6] *Persi.*
[7] Cf. Lk 16.22.
[8] *Napersnikov.* Cf. Jn 13.23.
[9] Cf. Jn 19.34.

Rejoice, blood most priceless, unstintingly poured out for our
    sake from all the veins and parts of the Savior, and even
    from the very heart.
Rejoice, soul of Christ most holy, surrendered to God the
    Father with a mighty cry on our behalf on the cross.

In this very surrender, even I today surrender my soul unto you,
my Savior and Redeemer, and also all my feelings and words, my
counsels and intentions, and all the needs of my soul and body; my
faith and my station in life, the course and end of my life, the day
and hour of my last breath, my end and repose, and the resurrection
of my soul and body do I commend to you, and I pray you: receive
me into the hands of your protection as Master, and bless me with
your crucified palms, keep me in your wounds and deliver me from
every evil; by your blood cleanse the great multitude of my lawless
deeds; with your cross, as with a lance, pierce my cursed heart, that
apart from you, my life-giver, it should love no other, and that it
should always gaze upon you, crucified, and be sympathetic and
tender, fleeing from sin as from filthy vomit,[10] cutting off its own
will, laying all of itself upon your providence, and hoping thereby to
be of some use; by your death slay the soul-corrupting passions of
my body, and grant correction to my evil and dissolute life, shielding
me from approaching violent falls into sin, protecting my infirmity
from demons, passions, and human evil, and leading me along the
untroubled and saving path toward you, my haven and the consum-
mation of my desires; and numbering me with your blessed flock,
that, together with them, I may glorify you, my Creator, together
with the Father and the Holy Spirit, unto the ages. Amen.

[10]Cf. Prov 26.11, 2 Pet 2.22.

3
Worship of the Most Pure Mysteries of Christ

Divinity of Christ! Shine on me, have mercy on me![1]
Soul of Christ! Show me your loving-kindness, save me!
Body of Christ! Feed me, strengthen me!
Blood of Christ! Sate me, hallow me!
Water from the side of Christ! Wash me, purify me!
Painful suffering and death of Christ! Heal me, enliven me!
Cross of Christ! By your power guard me, enliven me, and
    overshadow my head on the day of battle!
O most sweet Jesus! Sweeten my heart with your love and hide
    me in your most holy wounds!
O most beloved Lover of mine! Do not separate yourself from
    me, and do not allow me to be separated from you, even
    for a short time!
O my all-powerful Deliverer! Deliver me from my enemies!
O most merciful ruler and guide of my life! Guide my paths
    toward salvation, and in the hour of my death send unto
    me good protectors and command my sinful soul to
    meekly depart from my cursed body. Protect me from the
    spirits of the air[2] and, at your dread judgment, separate me
    not from the portion on the right, that I may glorify your
    exceedingly great loving-kindness, together with all who
    glorify you, unto the ages. Amen.

[1]The opening lines of the work are a Slavonic paraphrase and expansion of the
well-known Latin *Anima Christi* prayer.
[2]Cf. Eph 2.2, 6.12.

After the fraction of the parts of Christ's body:

You have prepared a table before me in the presence of them
that harass me; you have anointed my head with oil; your
cup intoxicates me, for it is strong.[3]

After the usual prayer before communion, say mentally:

Lift up, you gates and bolts of my heart, and let the King of
glory enter.[4]

Enter, my light, and enlighten my darkness! Enter, my life, and
raise my deadness!

Enter, my physician, and heal my wounds! Enter, divine fire,
consume the thorns of my sins, burn up my inner parts
and my heart with the flame of your love! Enter, my King,
and uproot the kingdom of sin within me, sit upon the
throne of my heart and reign within me, you who alone are
my King and Lord!

After tasting the body of Christ:

How sweet is the God of Israel to the upright in heart! And
how sweet is Christ to those who love him sweetly!
Sweeten me with your love, most sweet Jesus!

Before the holy cup:

What shall I render unto the Lord for all he has rendered unto
me? I shall receive the cup of salvation and call on the
name of the Lord.[5]

---

[3]Cf. Ps 22.5. This psalm is a part of the pre-communion rule contemporary in
Orthodox prayer books, both Greek and Russian.

[4]Cf. Ps 23.7–9. This psalm is likewise a part of the pre-communion rule in contemporary prayer books.

[5]Ps 115.3–4.

After tasting the blood of Christ:

You are all desire, all sweetness,[6] Word of God, Son of the
   Virgin, God of gods, Lord, Most Holy of holies. You and
   the one who bore you do we magnify.

Bow to the earth and say, "Glory to you, O God," *thrice. And then the
usual prayers of thanksgiving. And afterward say the following:*

Magnitude of my soul, rejoicing of my spirit, sweetness of my heart,
most sweet Jesus, my glory which lifts up my head,[7] be with me and
in me inseparably always, and with your all-powerful right hand
hold me with you and in you, that I may cling to you,[8] my Lord, in
one spirit[9] together with you; that all my thoughts, words, and intentions may be in you and for you and with you, for without you I can
do nothing;[10] [and] that I may live not for myself, but for you, my
Master and Benefactor;[11] that my senses of soul and body may labor
not for me, but for you, my Creator, by whom they live and move;[12]
that my powers of soul and body may serve you, my Redeemer, by
whom and in whom they are maintained; and that my whole life,
even to my last breath, O God, may be unto the glory of your most
holy name. Amen.

To the Theotokos:

O most immaculate Mother of God, while remaining Ever-Virgin,
you gave flesh and blood to the Son of God from your most pure
and most holy womb. I thank you, that you have made even me,
who am unworthy, worthy to be a communicant[13] of this same flesh

---

[6] Cf. Song 5.16.
[7] Ps 3.4.
[8] Cf. Ps 62.9.
[9] Cf. 1 Cor 6.17.
[10] Cf. Jn 15.5.
[11] Cf. the second prayer of thanksgiving after communion in contemporary Russian prayer books. My thanks to Fr Ignatius Green for pointing out this reference.
[12] Cf. Acts 17.28.
[13] Cf. the final prayer of thanksgiving after communion in contemporary Russian
prayer books. Once again, my thanks to Fr Ignatius Green for pointing this out.

and blood, by communion of which I am united to your Son and my God. I believe and confess you to be the Mother of grace: make me never to be cast off all the days of my life. O the maternal mercy of your child-loving mercy! O this, my most sweet, divine table! You are like a life-giving ear of grain, who bore for the world a kernel of wheat: Christ. You are the vine cultivated by God, sprouting for us the ripened grape: Jesus. Feed me always with this incorruptible bread, and give me to drink ever of this life-creating drink, so that, tasting them now, under these accidents, and beholding how good is my God, how exceedingly beloved my Lover, how delightful my Lord, I may be made worthy, after this, to see him openly, face to face,[14] and also to delight in the sight of the most bright countenance of your own face, when your glory shall be made manifest unto me unto the ages.[15] Amen.

[14]Cf. 1 Cor 13.12.
[15]Cf. Ps 4.7; cf. also Ps 89.16–17.

4

Discerning Divine Communion, for Otherwise It Is Damnation to Oneself, Not Discerning the Lord's Body[1]

My Lord and my God, in the most pure mysteries is my
    healing. I am sick.
The Lord is my health. I am crushed, weakened, and barely
    alive.
The Lord is my cleansing. I am a leper.
The Lord is my life. I am dead.
The Lord is my shepherd. I am his lost sheep.[2]
The Lord is my rising. I am fallen.
The Lord is my acquittal. I am condemned.
The Lord seeks me. I am lost.[3]

And so I come forward, as one sick to a healer, so that I may be healed; as one crushed and weakened to a doctor, so that I may be cured; as one dead to my life, that I may rise from sinful death and live to virtue.

I come forward as a sheep to my shepherd, that I may be safe from the wolf;[4] as one fallen to the one who raises me up, that I may fall no more; as one condemned to my judge, that he may, by his own compassion, make me from unrighteous to righteous.

[1] 1 Cor 11.29.

[2] Cf. Lk 15.1–7, Jn 10.11 and 14; cf. also Ps 22.1, though in Slavonic (and in the Vulgate and Septuagint) the psalm reads in a way less familiar to English speakers: "The Lord shepherds me."

[3] Cf. Lk 19.10.

[4] Cf. Jn 10.11–15.

I come forward, as one lost to the one who seeks me, the lover of mankind, that I may abide ever with him and in him, and he with me and in me, that I may not live unto myself, but rather unto him, my Master and Benefactor,[5] for henceforth and already I no longer live, but rather Christ lives in me.[6]

I receive the most pure mysteries so that, finding help by communing of them, from now on I may lay down a good beginning of my salvation and no longer labor for sin, but, according to my strength, labor for my God, for by your cooperation and support, I believe, Lord my God, in your all-powerful help and goodness: "I believe, Lord, help my unbelief."[7]

Second Discerning. Healing in the Time of Despair.

What are my sins against your loving-kindness, Lord? They are a spider web against a great wind, they are a small swamp against a great river, they are darkness against the sun all bright.

A strong wind shall blow, and it shall tear the spider web. The river shall flow, and it shall wash away the swamp.[8] The sun shall shine, and it shall chase away the darkness.

And so it is meet that your surpassingly great loving-kindness, God, tear up my sins, like a wind a spider web; wash away my transgressions, like a river a swamp; enlighten me, like the sun the darkness; and chase away all my evil deeds, words, and intentions. Your right hand receives me, who return like the prodigal son, in paternal embrace.[9]

And so why do I doubt? I shall not doubt in your goodness, I shall not despair, O my Lord; in your mercy, I shall never despair! In this I know you [to be] God, all-powerful and mighty: that my sins, and those of the whole world, shall never overcome your loving-kindness. If they were to overcome it, you would not be God, mighty and all-powerful.

[5]Cf. second of the Prayers of Thanksgiving (the "Post-Communion Prayers").
[6]Gal 2.20.
[7]Mk 9.24.
[8]For these two lines, cf. Ps 147.7.
[9]Cf. Lk 15.11–32.

5

Worship of the Most Holy Theotokos

Come, let us worship our Queen, the Theotokos.[1]
Come, let us worship the Virgin Mary, our Queen, the
    Theotokos.
Come, let us worship and fall down before the Lady[2] Virgin
    Mary herself, our Queen, the Theotokos.

I worship you, Most Holy Virgin, who have, by your birthgiving, revealed to us the true light. O Queen of heaven and earth, hope of the hopeless, helper of the helpless, and intercessor for all sinners, cover me and protect me from all afflictions and necessities of soul and body, and be for me, I pray, a protector, through your holy prayers.

I worship your sinless conception[3] and birth from your holy parents Joachim and Anne, and I pray you, my Lady: grant me to conceive a sinless life, and to give birth to repentance.

I worship your entrance into the church[4] of the Lord as a child three years old, and I pray you, my light, make me a church of the Holy Spirit,[5] through your prayers.

---

[1]A variant on part of the common beginning to Orthodox liturgical services: "Come, let us worship God our King. Come let us worship Christ God, our King. Come, let us worship and fall down before Christ God himself, our King."

[2]The "Lady" here matches the word "Lord," printed as part of *Come, Let us Worship* in Russian service books before the time of Patriarch Nikon. The word "Lord" is absent in the post-Nikonian version of the text..

[3]See above, pp. 16–18, 21, and 35–36.

[4]In the Slavonic translation of scriptural texts, the Jerusalem temple is frequently called a "church" (*tserkov'*) rather than a temple (*khram*).

[5]Cf. 1 Cor 6.19.

I worship your annunciation, Most Pure Virgin, when, by the action of the Holy Spirit, together with archangel's voice, you conceived the Word of the Father. And I pray you, my light, announce salvation unto me, who am in despair.

I worship your birthgiving, when you incarnated and bore Christ, the Savior of the world, and when you were glorified and exalted by all creation as the Mother of God, and I pray you, my light: reveal yourself to me as a loving-kind Mother both now and in the future age.

I worship your purification, O undefiled, unsullied, incorrupt, and most holy one, and I pray you, my light: cleanse me from every defilement of flesh and spirit through your prayers.

I worship and honor your pains[6] that you endured at the time of the voluntary Passion of your Son, when the prophecy of Simeon came to pass: "A sword shall pierce your own soul also";[7] and I pray you, my light: deliver me from pains of soul and body.

I worship you, Lady, recalling your joy, which you had at the time of the resurrection of your Son, and I pray you, my light: deprive me not of spiritual joys.

I worship your honorable and glorious dormition,[8] and I pray you, my light: by your aid, lay to rest[9] the passions of my flesh.

Most holy Lady Theotokos, receive this small supplication, and bring it before your Son and our God, that he may save and enlighten our souls for your sake. Gazing on your most holy image as if on you, your true self, the Theotokos, I fall down with heartfelt faith and with love from my soul, [and] I worship you, together with the pre-eternal infant whom you hold in your arms, our Lord Jesus Christ, and I honor him in God-befitting manner, and I pray you

---

[6]*Bolezni*. This could also be translated "sorrows" or "afflictions," and such a translation would highlight the parallels between St Dimitri's veneration here and the veneration afforded the Seven Sorrows of Mary by Latin Christians.

[7]Lk 2.35.
[8]*Uspenie*.
[9]*Upsi*.

with tears: cover[10] me with your veil[11] from enemies both visible and invisible, for you have led the race of man into the kingdom of heaven. Amen.

And then: It is truly meet.[12]

[10]*Pokryj.*

[11]Slavonic *pokrov.* This word can mean both covering or veil (from the verb *pokryti,* appearing here in the imperative and translated "cover"; see immediately above) and, by extension, protection. Consequently, the word refers both to the Theotokos' veil and to her protection, or perhaps to her veil as a symbol of her protection, the feast of which, celebrated in the Russian Church on October 1, is also called *Pokrov.*

[12]The incipit of the well-known prayer, common to many Orthodox liturgical services: "It is truly meet to bless you, the Theotokos, ever-blessed, most immaculate, and the Mother of our God. More honorable than the cherubim and more glorious beyond compare than the seraphim, without corruption bearing God the Word [or, the God Word], being the Theotokos, we magnify you." Cf. the less literal translation in *Divine Liturgy,* 70.

6
Worship of the Holy Trinity

All the powers of my soul:

Come, let us worship God, one in Trinity, Father, Son, and Holy Spirit.

All the thoughts of my heart:

Come, let us worship the Trinity, honored in unity.

All the senses of my body:

Come, let us worship and fall down and lament before the Lord, who created us.[1]

I worship you, most holy, life-creating Trinity, one in essence and undivided, Father, Son, and Holy Spirit: I believe in you and I confess, glorify, thank, praise, honor, [and] exalt you, and I pray: have mercy on me, your unworthy servant. *Thrice.*

I worship you, God the Father, for you have brought me from non-being into being [and] adorned me with your divine image.[2]

I worship you, God the Son, for you have obtained me by your precious blood, you have redeemed me from the curse of the law,[3] [and] you have enlightened me by holy baptism.

I worship you, God the Holy Spirit, for you have enlivened me, given me reason, [and] made me radiant by the light of faith.

---

[1] Another prayer based on the traditional *Come, Let Us Worship.* Cf. above, p. 57, footnote 1.

[2] Cf. Gen 1.27.

[3] Cf. Gal 3.13.

I worship you, God the Father, for you have given me a soul by
   your divine and life-creating inbreathing.

I worship you, God the Son, for on the cross you have laid
   down your soul for me.[4]

I worship you, God the Holy Spirit, for you deliver my
   soul from death, my eyes from tears, and my legs from
   feebleness.[5]

I worship you, God the Father, for you do not destroy me, who
   have sinned, together with my lawless deeds, but you suffer
   long, awaiting my return.

I worship you, God the Son, for you do not desire the death of
   me, a sinner,[6] but in your loving-kindness you call me to
   repentance.

I worship you, God the Holy Spirit, for you do not despise me
   who return, you do not push away me who fall, but rather
   you receive me as the prodigal son,[7] and you renew a right
   spirit within my bowels.[8]

I worship you, God the Father, cleansing all my transgressions.[9]

I worship you, God the Son, healing all my illnesses.[10]

I worship you, God the Holy Spirit, delivering my life from
   corruption.[11]

I worship you, God the Father, who are not angry unto the end,
   nor hostile unto the ages.[12]

I worship you, God the Son, who do not do unto me according
   to my transgressions.[13]

---

[4]Cf. Jn 10.17–18, 15.13.
[5]Ps 55.14.
[6]Cf. Ezek 18.23, 33.11.
[7]Lk 15.11–32.
[8]Ps 50.12
[9]Ps 102.3.
[10]Ps 102.4.
[11]Ps 102.5.
[12]Ps 102.9.
[13]Ps 102.10.

I worship you, God the Holy Spirit, who do not render unto
    me according to my sins.[14]

I worship you, God the Father, who have compassion on me as
    a father has compassion on his sons.[15]

I worship you, God the Son, who know my passionate nature
    and weakness.

I worship you, God the Holy Spirit, who heal my infirmities
    and cleanse me from every defilement.

I worship you, God the Father, for you set me aright, who am
    fallen.

I worship you, God the Son, for you seek me, who am lost.

I worship you, God the Holy Spirit, for you enliven me, who
    am dead.

I worship you, God the Father, loving-kind, my hope.

I worship you, God the Son, long-suffering, my refuge.

I worship you, God the Holy Spirit, desiring no evil, my
    protector.[16]

Falling to the ground, say this:

Truly it is meet[17] for me to worship, doxologize, and thank you,
O Holy Trinity, whom the heavenly powers, the cherubim and

---

[14] Ps 102.10.

[15] Ps 102.13.

[16] These lines are based on a prayer attributed to St Ioannicius, part of the Eastern Orthodox Compline service: "My hope is the Father, my refuge is the Son, my protector is the Holy Spirit. Holy Trinity, glory to you."

[17] Cf. the traditional Marian hymn *It is Truly Meet*. Cf. above, p. 59, footnote 12. This particular hymn has a prior history of adaptation: a version addressed to Christ, ascribed to St Gregory of Sinai, appears in the Eastern Orthodox Midnight Office for Sundays throughout the year (pre-Nikonian books also include a second version, addressed to the Trinity and ascribed to the same), and versions addressed to the Holy Spirit and the Trinity appear at the end of the *Supplicatory Canon to the Divine and Worshipped Paraclete, [which] we Sing at the Third Hour of the Day with an Alert Mind, not Darkened by Gluttony or Drunkenness*, attributed to St Maximus the Greek. Concerning the attribution of this latter work, see G. A. Kazimova, " 'Kanon moleben k bozhestvennomu i poklanjaemomu Paraklity' prepodobnogo Maksima Greka: k voprosu ob atributsii i funktsional'noj transformatsii [*The Supplicatory Canon to the Divine and Worshipped Paraclete*, by St Maximus the Greek: Toward the Question

seraphim, praise with thrice-holy hymns, whom all the saints thank, whom all of creation worships, as it befits servants to do; and I, a mortal, crawling worm, deprived of boldness before the greatness of your unapproachable glory, dare to hope upon your mercy, [and] shamelessly I fall down and pray: grant me always to worship you, my Creator, uncondemned and without laziness, to know you alone, to love and fear you, to keep your precepts, to walk the path of your commandments, to praise and glorify you to my last breath; and after my separation from my mortal body, and my new unity with it, do not deprive me of crying out joyously unto the ages, together with those who have pleased you, "Holy, holy, holy." Amen.

of Attribution and Functional Transformation]," *Vestnik Obshchestva issledovatelej Drevnej Rusi za 2002–2003 gg.* [*Newsletter of the Society of Scholars of Old Russia for the Years 2002–2003*] (Moscow: Institut mirovoj literatury im. A. M. Gor'kogo RAN, 2007), 281–94.

7
Worship of Jesus Christ

Come, let us worship . . . *Thrice.*[1]

Son of God, I worship your birth from the Father, without a mother,[2] before the morning star,[3] and your ineffable watching over us.

I worship your mysterious condescension for our salvation, Lord and lover of mankind: the incarnation in the womb of a Virgin through the activity of the Holy Spirit, the birth, and the deposition[4] in a manger for cattle.

I worship and glorify your fleshly circumcision, humble baptism by a servant, most bright transfiguration on Tabor, glorious triumphal movement into Jerusalem unto voluntary suffering, [and] all your labors undertaken upon the earth for our sake, during which you were fasting from your youth and struggling, moving and working, teaching and preaching, healing and raising [the dead]: recalling all these things, I glorify, magnify, honor, and kiss you with love, and for all of this I thank you, my Creator, exceedingly loving-kind.

I worship your mystical supper, O Son of God, at which you gave your very self as food to believers, so that, communing of your body and blood, I may possess your eternal life. I magnify also your profound humility revealed in the washing of your disciples' feet,

---

[1] For the full text of this prayer, see above, p. 57, footnote 1.

[2] This echoes the language of any number of patristic and liturgical texts, in particular the theotokia at "Lord, I have cried" and at the aposticha at Great Vespers, in the third tone, on Saturday evenings. My thanks to Fr Ignatius Green for pointing this out to me.

[3] Cf. Ps 109.3.

[4] *Polozhenie.* Note that this word is one traditionally used for the entombment of Christ by Sts Joseph and Nicodemus.

and I pray you, my Lord: humble my exalted pride and teach me humility of mind.

I worship your most pure, most holy, and life-creating body, broken for me under the appearance of bread for the remission of sins.[5]

I worship your most pure, most holy, and life-creating blood, poured out under the appearance of wine for the remission of sins.[6]

I worship your sufferings, O Christ. *Thrice.*[7]

I worship your bowing of knees in the garden, where, praying, you poured out bloody sweat so that the cup of suffering might pass from you.[8] I pray you, my Lord, teach me to pray fervently always, and give me to drink of the cup of salvation,[9] that I may thank you unto the ages.

I worship you, my Lord and my God, recalling your voluntary suffering: the deceitful kiss of Judas, the guiltless arrest by lawless people, the binding and countless insults, blows, spitting, abuse, vexations, beatings, agony, abasement, [and] all your torments that you endured for the sake of me, who am a wretch and an ingrate, and also the pitiless spilling of blood. All these I lay up in my mind and heart, with love I kiss them, I melt with pity, and for all of this I exalt and thank you, my beloved Lord, who have so loved me that you did not hesitate to lay down even your own soul for me.[10]

I worship your guiltless condemnation to death, my Judge, your painful bearing of the heavy cross, the stretching out of your most pure body upon the cross, the nailing and the crucifixion on

[5]Cf. Mt 26.26 and parallels, and also 26.28, and also and especially the words of institution as given in the eucharistic anaphora of St John Chrysostom.

[6]Cf. Mt 26.27–28 and parallels, and again and especially the eucharistic anaphora of St John of Chrysostom.

[7]Cf. the refrains before and after the Gospel at matins on Holy Friday, and also the the fifteenth antiphon sung at the same service.

[8]Cf. Lk 22.44.

[9]Cf. Ps 115.4.

[10]Jn 10.17–18, 15.13.

Golgotha in between two thieves. And I pray you, my Lord, do not judge me according to my deeds, grant me to bear my cross without laziness, nail down my flesh with your fear,[11] crucify me to the world with its passions and lusts,[12] and grant me that my heart may know nothing else all the days of my life, except for you, Jesus crucified.[13]

I worship your most pure and most holy head, slashed with a sharp crown of thorns for the sake of me, an ingrate, and I pray you, my Lord: uproot from my head those things which are evil, defiled, prodigal, blasphemous, and vainglorious.

I worship your most holy ears, filled with impious blasphemy for the sake of me, a wretch and an ingrate, and I pray you, my Lord: grant me to hear nothing useless and make me obedient to your precept.

I worship your most pure eyes, which flowed with tears and blood for the sake of me, a wretch and an ingrate, and I pray you, my Lord: look on me and have mercy on me, and open my eyes to see no vanity.[14]

I worship your most pure face, which shone like the sun on Tabor, but which is now darkened by spitting and slapping, and I pray you, my Lord: shine your face upon your servant.[15]

I worship your most pure mouth and tongue, burning with thirst, which tasted gall and vinegar, and I pray you, my Lord: curb my evil tongue, and set a guard over my mouth.[16]

I worship your most pure, most holy, and life-creating wound on your right hand, and I pray you, my Lord: make me worthy to stand at your right hand.[17]

---

[11]"Nailing down" the passions, the flesh, and so on, is a common image from Orthodox liturgical prayer: cf., e.g., the prayer at the conclusion of the sixth hour.

[12]Cf. Gal 5.24.

[13]Cf. 1 Cor 2.2.

[14]Ps 118.37.

[15]Ps 118.35.

[16]Ps 140.3.

[17]Cf. Mt 25.33.

I worship your most pure, most holy, and life-creating wound on your left hand, and I pray you, my Lord: deliver me from the lefthand portion.[18]

I worship your most pure, most holy, and life-creating wound on your right[19] foot, and I pray you, my Lord: establish me on the upright[19] path of repentance.

I worship your most pure, most holy, and life-creating wound on your left foot, and I pray you, my Lord: forbid my feet from every wicked path.[21]

I worship your most pure, most holy, and life-creating wound on your most pure side and in your pierced heart, from which flowed out blood and water[22] for our redemption, and I pray you, my Lord: crush my stoniness, smite my cruel heart, guard it with your fear, wound it with your love, so that I may love you, my Lord, with all my heart, all my soul, all my thought, all my might and all my intention,[23] and so that springs of tears may flow from my broken heart, washing away my sinful defilement.

I worship your whole holy body, wounded from the feet to the head for the sake of me, a wretch and an ingrate, and which has no wholeness, and I pray you, my Lord: heal me, who am all wounded by sins.

I worship the nakedness of your most pure body, and I pray you, my Lord: cover the filthy nakedness of my wretched soul.[24]

I worship your most holy soul, surrendered into the hands of God the Father,[25] and I pray you, my Lord: receive my soul into your holy hands at the hour of its departure and keep it from the aerial spirits of evil.[26]

[18]Cf. Mt 25.33.
[19]*Desnyj.*
[20]Or, "right." *Pravyj.*
[21]Ps 118.101.
[22]Cf. Jn 19.34.
[23]Deut 6.5; cf. also Lk 10.27 and Mt 22.37.
[24]Cf. perhaps Ezek 16.8, Hos 2.9, or Gen 9.23.
[25]Cf. Lk 23:46.
[26]Cf. Eph 2.2, 6.12.

I worship your most pure body's deposition from the cross and placement in the tomb, and I pray you, my Lord: grant me that I may live in the world as one dead and buried.

Glory to your sufferings, O Lord![27] *Thrice.*

I worship, doxologize, and magnify your descent into hell, captivity of hell, trampling down of death, and third-day resurrection from the tomb, and I pray you, my Lord: capture my soul, captured by sins, with your love; raise it, which is dead; and deliver it from hell.

Glory, O Lord, to your cross and resurrection![28]

I worship your ascension with your flesh into heaven, where, sitting at the right hand of God the Father, you see my poverty and infirmity, you hear my sinful prayer, you understand my intentions from afar, and you know my address [to you]. So I pray you, my Lord: raise my mind up from earthly predilection to the desire on high, make mighty my infirmity, make up for my inadequacy and meagerness, guide my prayer, and lead me to a good end and the haven of salvation, that I may appear before you unashamed and uncondemned when you come to judge the living and the dead. Lord, do not enter into judgment with your servant, for no one living shall be counted righteous before you.[29]

Falling down to the ground, say the following:

It is truly meet[30] to worship you, my Lord Jesus Christ, God glorified and worshipped by all the saints, at whose name every knee shall bow, in heaven, and on earth, and under the earth.[31] And also I, the unworthy, shamelessly approach and pray: save me, my Savior, according to your goodness, and not according to my deeds. You wish to save me, you know how to save me, as you wish, as you can,

[27] Cf. above, p. 66, footnote, 7.
[28] This is the refrain for hymnographic canons to the cross and the resurrection, part of the usual Sunday Matins service in the Russian Orthodox tradition.
[29] Ps 142.2.
[30] Cf. above, p. 59, footnote 12, and also p. 63, footnote 17.
[31] Phil 2.10.

as you know: by the judgments you know, save me. I hope on you,
my Lord, and I hand myself over to your holy will: do with me as
you wish. If you wish to have me in light, may you be blessed. If you
wish to have me in darkness, again, may you be blessed. If you open
to me the doors of your loving-kindness, this is well and good. If you
close to me the doors of your loving-kindness, blessed are you, Lord,
who have closed them to me according to your righteousness. If you
do not destroy me together with my transgressions, glory to your
measureless loving-kindness. If you destroy me together with my
transgressions, glory to your righteous judgment. Arrange things
for me as you wish.

8

Excerpts from
Spiritual Therapy for Confusion of Thoughts, Collected in a Brief Form from Various Patristic Books

Prayers for Deliverance from Blasphemous Thoughts

First Prayer

God before the ages, witness of hidden things, who try hearts and reins, who sit on the cherubim and behold the abysses, and who comprehend my intentions from afar, you know that I hate, I do not want, and I do not will these impure, filthy, blasphemous thoughts which beset me shamelessly, and I pray your goodness: forbid the spirit of blasphemy, so that he depart from me; drive away evil thoughts, lest they torment me; quiet the tumult of my heart; make meek the storm of my thoughts; put the enemy, who troubles my conscience, to shame, lest my enemy rejoice over me; for all the opposing spirits tremble and shake before you, all things obey you, all things have labored for you; command the storms and tumult in my mind, and let it turn into silence, so that without doubt and confusion I may labor for you, my Lord, throughout all the days of my life. Amen.

Second Prayer

Lord, you see my sorrow, you see my affliction, you see the shame-lessness of my enemy, how violently and heavily he besets me with blasphemous thoughts, sorrowing my soul, causing sorrow to my heart, darkening my mind, and troubling my conscience. His God-blaspheming whispering and filthy-to-God chattering in mind I hate so much that I would rather die than accept these blasphemous thoughts against you, my good God, and consent to these things that my enemy goes on announcing in my mind, but on account of my weakness I am unable to chase from myself and overcome these opposing and God-blaspheming and filthy-to-God thoughts without your help, my God, for my nature is passionate, my mind inconstant, my power feeble, but my opponent mighty, and his power exceeds my power; and if you, Lord, were not mighty and strong among your people, then who could be sufficient to be kept whole against the enemy, the devil, the murderer of mankind? Therefore I fall down before you, O all-merciful and most loving-kind, who do not desire my despair, Creator, God, and I pray your all-powerful help: smite on the head the enemy who troubles me,[1] flash lightning and scatter the opponents who have surrounded me,[2] shining a bright ray of your grace in my heart, so that the dark cloud of blasphemous thoughts found over me may flee from me; so that I may behold you, my Christ, who enlighten every man,[3] in the light of your help; so that I may enter into the light of your countenance and rejoice in your name unto the ages.[4] Amen.

Third Prayer, against the Demon of Blasphemy

May your pain return upon your [own] head, and may your blas-phemy come down on top of you, O wicked and unclean demon; for I worship the Lord my God and shall never blaspheme him.

[1]Cf. perhaps Ps 67.22.
[2]Cf. Ps 17.15 (also 2 Sam 22.15).
[3]Cf. Jn 1.9.
[4]Cf. Ps 4.7.

How could I possibly vex or blaspheme him whom I worship and doxologize throughout every day and every night, and throughout the hours, with all my soul and might and my thought? Rather, therefore, doxology is mine, but blasphemy is yours; you shall see: [it is] you [who] blapheme against him concerning these things, and speak against God as an apostate.

Fourth prayer

The Lord, who came into the world through the most pure Virgin, [who is] truly Theotokos, for the salvation of the world, on account of us sinners, forbids you, all-wicked spirit, the devil. You are cursed, and also all your unwelcome intentions, which [come] during the night and during the day. I adjure you by the name of the Trinity, one in essence and undivided, Father and Son and Holy Spirit: depart from me, the servant of God (*name*), do not lay up unwelcome thoughts in my heart, but rather go out into empty and waterless places[5] where the Lord does not visit. I adjure you, unclean and God-blaspheming spirit, by the name of our Lord Jesus Christ, neither to tempt nor trouble me with blasphemous thoughts when I make my prayers to the Lord my God, but rather may all your blasphemous intentions be on your [own] head on judgment day, for I serve my Lord and to him alone do I send up prayer day and night, he who harnesses you and has mercy on me, and makes me mighty, and who looses all my transgressions on account of his great goodness. Get behind me, Satan, and be you cursed, and also your unwelcome and opposing power, for blessed and glorified be the most honorable name of the Father and of the Son and of the Holy Spirit, now and ever, and unto ages of ages. Amen.

Fifth Prayer, to the Most Pure Theotokos

My most holy Lady Theotokos, by your holy and all-powerful supplications drive away from me, your wretched servant, despondency,

[5] Cf. Mt 12.43. My thanks to Fr Ignatius Green for catching this reference.

forgetfulness, senselessness, indifference, and all filthy, wicked, and blasphemous intentions, from my wretched heart and my darkened mind, and quench the flame of my passions, for I am poor and wretched, and deliver me from many violent recollections and undertakings, and free me from all evil activites. For you are blessed from all generations and your most honorable name is glorified unto the ages. Amen.

Sixth Prayer, to God

Into the hands of your loving-kindness most great, O my God, I commend my soul and body,[6] my senses and words, my counsels and thoughts, my deeds and all the uses of my soul and body, my entrance into and departure from [this life], my faith and station in life, the course and end of my life, the day and hour of my last breath, death and repose, and the resurrection of my soul and body with all your chosen saints. And so do you, most good God who loves mankind, receive me into the hands of your protection and deliver me from every evil; forgive the exceeding multitude of my sins, cleanse my defiled soul and body, and keep me under the shelter of your mercy throughout all the days of my life, so that I, made mighty by your grace, may be delivered from the enemy's nets that snare me and, led into sense by your charity and established on the path of true repentance, be made worthy of a Christian end to my life, passionless, unashamed, peaceful and untroubled by the arrival of aerial spirits; and of a good answer at your dread judgment, and that I may be worthy of beholding your unspeakable glory and hearing your most sweet, blessed voice; and that I may receive life and salvation from you, my God. Amen.

After this, read Psalm 26: "The Lord is my enlightenment and my savior."[7] *Then,* "It is truly meet,"[8] *and the dismissal.*

If possible, also perform bows according to your strength, and, God helping, you shall be delivered from blasphemous thoughts.

[6]Cf. Lk 23.46.
[7]Ps 26.1.
[8]Cf. above, p. 59, footnote 12.

A VERY BRIEF METHOD FOR DEFEATING
BLASPHEMOUS THOUGHTS

If there should arise a blasphemous thought against God, read, "I believe in one God . . . ,"[9] to the end. And if it be possible, make however many metanias or bows[10] according to your strength.

If there should arise a blasphemous thought against the most pure mysteries of Christ, read, "I believe, O Lord, and I confess, that you are truly the Christ . . . ,"[11] to the end, and make bows.

If there should arise a blasphemous thought against the most pure Theotokos, then read some prayer to the Most Pure Theotokos, either "Beneath your compassion . . . ,"[12] or "Theotokos, Virgin, rejoice . . . ,"[13] or some other troparion to the Theotokos, with bows, saying, "Most Holy Theotokos, save me, a sinner."[14]

If there should arise a blasphemous thought against some certain saint, read, "Saint (*name*), pray to God for me, a sinner, for after God

[9]That is, the Nicene-Constantinopolitan Creed.

[10]Though the term "bow" (*poklon*) can potentially mean either a bow to the ground (*poklon do zemli, zemnyj poklon*) or from the waist (*pojasnyj poklon*), here the former is clearly meant, since "metania" always refers to the latter.

[11]A ubiquitous pre-communion prayer: "I believe, Lord, and I confess, that you are truly the Christ, the Son of the Living God, come into the world to save sinners, of whom I am the first. Also, I believe that this is truly your own most pure body, and that this is your own precious blood. Therefore I pray you, have mercy on me, and forgive all my transgressions, both voluntary and involuntary, both in word and in deed, committed in knowledge and in ignorance, and make me worthy to partake uncondemned of your most pure mysteries, for the remission of my sins, and unto life everlasting." Cf. the translation, upon which mine was based, in *Divine Liturgy*, 80–81.

[12]The prayer known in Latin as *Sub tuum Praesidium*: "Beneath your compassion we flee, Virgin Theotokos. Despise not our prayers in our afflictions, but deliver us from sorrows, only pure and blessed one."

[13]The angelic salutation: "Theotokos, Virgin, rejoice: Mary, full of grace, the Lord is with you. Blessed are you among women, and blessed is the fruit of your womb, for you have borne the Savior of our souls." In the Orthodox tradition, this prayer appears in slightly different forms, but this one has become standard in the Russian Church. See also above, p. 45, footnote 1.

[14]This is another familiar prayer, derived from the liturgical formula "Most holy Theotokos, save us."

I flee unto you, a swift helper and intercessor for our souls," and do
bows according to your strength, saying, "Saint (*name*), pray to God
for me, a sinner."

If there should arise a blasphemous thought against some certain
icon, make fifteen bows before this icon, or however many you can
manage, praying to the one depicted on this icon, and in this way,
with God's help, you will in no way return to blasphemous thoughts.
Amen.

9

A Godly Contemplative Meditation on the Most Holy Sufferings of Our Lord Jesus Christ

Every truly believing son of the Church should recall the death of Christ, which he endured in the flesh for our sake without guilt, for he committed no sin, and there was no lying in his mouth.[1] Therefore, O God-loving soul, be thankful to the one who suffered and died for your sake. Take up the beginning, starting from the timeless birth of the Son of God, meditating with faith alone on his unsearchable, ineffable, and incomprehensible birth from the Father before the ages, and how the Word of God—born before the ages from the Father, the priceless treasure of the Father's heart, whom the Father bore from the womb before the morning star[2]—[how] the very Word of God, the most beloved Son of God the Father, consented, by the good will of the Father and the co-activity of the Holy Spirit, for the sake of our salvation to take up human nature and to arrange our salvation in it. He was born from the most immaculate Virgin Mary in time, he took up human nature from her most pure blood, he created for this nature a rational soul, he became a perfect man, and with respect to this humanity he grew up to a perfect stature.[3] When the fore-appointed time of our redemption arrived, then Christ, our Savior and God, at his mystical supper, handed down a most terrible

[1] 1 Pet 2.2 (cf. Is 53.9).

[2] Cf. Ps 109.3.

[3] Cf. Lk 2.52 and Eph 4.13. I thank Fr Ignatius Green for pointing out the second of these allusions, which helped me to recognize the first.

and most dread mystery to his disciples and apostles, and through them even to us, for taking bread in his most exceedingly holy and divine hands, blessing it, he broke it and gave it to his disciples and apostles, saying, "Take, eat. This is my body."[4] Giving thanks for this beneficence, everyone ought to say the Lord's Prayer, "Our Father,"[5] with this ending: "For yours is the kingdom and the power and the glory,[6] together with your unoriginate Father and your Most Holy and good and life-creating Spirit, now, and ever, and unto ages of ages. Amen."[7] And a bow.

And at this, his mystical supper, Christ, the Son of God, taking the cup in his most divine and most holy hands, offering praise, gave it to his disciples, saying, "Drink from it, all of you: this is my blood of the New Testament, which is poured out for you and for many for the remission of sins."[8] Giving thanks for this beneficence, that Christ our Savior made us worthy of these most dread mysteries not on account of some service of ours, but rather on account of his own extreme and unspeakable mercy and love toward the human race, [and] that he looked down on our corrupted nature, and renewed again that which was fallen for the better, and recreated it, and reconciled it to himself, and made us of one blood and of one body—giving thanks for this, say the prayer "Our Father." And a bow.

After the mystical supper, Christ, the Son of God, out of his exceedingly deep humility and ineffable love, standing up from the supper, laid down his garments and, taking a towel, girded himself. Then, pouring water into a washbasin, he began to wash his disciples' feet and dry them with the towel with which he was girt.[9] Wondering at his exceedingly deep humility and strange appearance, let

---

[4]Mt 26.26.

[5]Cf. Mt 6.9–12.

[6]Mt 16.13b.

[7]Note, given the form of the doxology ("your Father . . . your . . . Spirit"), that St Dimitri here takes the Lord's Prayer to be addressed to Christ rather than the Father. This remains apparent throughout the work.

[8]Mt 26.27–28.

[9]Cf. Jn 13.4–5.

everyone try to read the prayer "Our Father" with tenderness of heart. And a bow.

Then Christ, the Son of God, went out with his disciples to the Mount of Olives, according to his custom, and, bowing his knees there, he prayed to God the Father, saying, "Father, if you be well disposed, pass this cup away from me! However, not what I will, but what you [will]; your will be done."[10] He prayed three times,[11] and was in struggle: fervently he prayed! And his sweat became like great drops of blood dripping down to the ground.[12] Recalling this, his fervent prayer, let even us try to pray to him with great attentiveness and say, "Our Father." And a bow.

Here it befits this godly contemplation to consider [the following]: then the traitor Judas came with the given sign, with the soldiers who were sent with him: "He whom I kiss, this is he."[13] Our Savior and Redeemer, seeing his main enemy and traitor coming up to kiss him deceitfully, said, "Judas, do you betray the Son of Man with a kiss?"[14] Then the soldiers, binding him, dragged him away like an evildoer, and they led him first to Annas, for he was Caiaphas' father-in-law, and he was interrogated concerning his teaching and disciples. Jesus answered, "I spoke to the world directly. I always taught in the synagogue and the temple where the Jews always come together, and I said nothing secretly. Behold, these know what I said to them." And when he said this, one of the hearers standing nearby struck Jesus on the cheek, saying, "Is this how you answer the high priest?"[15] On account of such a great and inhuman blow, our Christ fell; he was not able to remain standing. He fell. O wonder! Our Savior fell. Our hope fell from this powerful blow, enduring for us this violent pain in accordance with his endless love for us. And then much blood flowed from his most holy mouth, from his nose, and

[10]Cf. Lk 22.39–44.
[11]Cf. Mt 26.39, 42, 44.
[12]Cf. Lk 22.44.
[13]Lk 22.48.
[14]Lk 22.48.
[15]Jn 18.13, 18–22.

from his ears on account of such an inhuman and merciless blow. Indeed this blow was heard throughout the whole high-priestly house. But, at this, to the one who slapped him he meekly answered these words: "If I have spoken wrongly, show what is wrong; but if [I have spoken] well, then why do you strike me?"[16] He said this as if [to say], "Why do you, O man, wound me, your Creator, so violently? Why do you harm my health [and] take away my life? Why do you place death before my eyes? Why do you make my dwelling in a tomb?" After such a powerful blow it would not have been possible to live, if humanity had not been made mighty by the power of divinity. Considering all these things, you, God-loving and Christ-loving soul, should, with bitter tears and tenderness of heart, bring to him the prayer, "Our Father." And a bow.

Holy godly contemplation, come once again behind Jesus, and see him bound to the pillar,[17] and there beaten and bloodied, all wounded, naked, and abused, blood flowing from his most holy wounded body, just as I said. But Jesus was silent, [and] for the sake of you, O man, he endured all of this with great disgrace and pain. The prophet Isaiah, seeing him suffering from afar, says, "And we saw him having neither appearance nor beauty."[18] One of the doctors testified this about him, interpreting the evangelical words:[19] " 'Behold the man!'[20] It was as if Pilate said, 'Look, ferocious Jewish race, on your king, who has not even the appearance of a man, but is rather all torn, bloodied, all in wounds; from feet to head there is no wholeness in him; know this and cease your fury. Should I not release for you him who is already sufficiently tortured?' But they cried, 'No. If you release him, you are not a friend of Caesar. Seize him, seize him, crucify him!' "[21] Contemplating this, bow down to

[16]Jn 18.23.
[17]Cf. Mk 15.15.
[18]Is 53.2.
[19]I have failed to identify the source of the quotation.
[20]Jn 19.5.
[21]Jn 19.12 and 15.

the earth, God-loving man, saying this prayer to the Son of God who suffers for you so violently: "Our Father." And a bow.

Holy godly contemplation, not much farther from the pillar, with noetic eyes see Christ, your Creator, Savior, and God, naked, in violent wounds beyond telling, trembling both from pain most extreme and from cold (for then it was winter[22]), putting his garment on himself. How great then, do you think, was the shame and dishonor with which the suffering Son of God was guiltlessly filled, stripped and wounded before all? O heaven! O earth! Senseless creation! Look and see your Creator, [and] how sensible and rational creation causes such great and unendurable offense to its Creator. Tarry no more, take up arms. Heaven, strike them with lightning and thunder. Sea, drown them with a dread flood. Sun, moon, and stars, and the rest of the fiery essence, carry out your activity, burn to ash those who are ungrateful and full of malice toward their benefactor. And you, earth, open your bowels, bring down into your depth not only the bodies but also the souls not only of those who commit the murder, but also those who are ungrateful for this suffering. And you, fiery kin, burn them unto endless ages with the fire of hell, and do not grant them relief for a short hour or a short interval, but always multiply [and] stretch long the ferocious torments. And this would have been done, had not God, suffering in the flesh, held it back with his all-accomplishing power, bearing the grave pains on account of love for the human race, for he desired the salvation of all, not their perishing. Therefore, if someone is a lover of Christ, let him, meditating on this, say to him the prayer, "Our Father." And a bow.

Holy godly contemplation and God-loving soul, remembering and considering these things, I pray you, do not stoop down to wordly vanity, which bears no benefit for you, but rather wait and be roused a little: look on the face of your Christ, and see with noetic eyes that it was not enough for malicious men to see him all wounded, but rather they took hold even of his face, already spat

[22]Cf. Jn 10.22.

upon, and they covered his face and struck it.[23] Certain doctors[24] of the Church, considering why they covered his most holy face, propose this: "Inasmuch as the face of Christ, our Savior and God, was filled with ineffable beauty, in accordance with the words of the Psalmist, 'Beautiful with comeliness above all the sons of mankind,'[25] and was filled tenderness, therefore they did not simply beat it, but also covered it, until they made the face itself disfigured, for it was all bruised and bloodied from violent blows."

Come and stand here, all sensible creation, and look on your King: can you know who this is? He is all mercilessly wounded, all in blood he has no appearance or comeliness,[26] and he suffers all this on account of your lack of self-control, for your sins have grievously wounded the King of glory. Therefore cease from now on to vex him, make peace through holy repentance, and do not again begin to wound your most beloved Redeemer, for he has suffered everything on account of your sins, in accordance with the prophecy spoken concerning him: "Taking up our sins, he was hurt for us, and we considered him to be pained, wounded, and afflicted by God. But he was wounded for our sins."[27] Considering this, say the prayer, "Our Father." And a bow.

And do not abandon godly contemplation yet, Christ-loving soul, but rather hear Christ the Savior speaking through the prophet: "All you who pass by along the way, look and see whether there is a pain so great as the pain which befell me."[28] Still this torment was not enough for the malicious Jews. Even though they saw his whole body was like one wound, nonetheless that malicious stepmother,[29] the assembly of the Jews, crowned his holy head with a crown made not from precious stone, but from thorns, and with prickly thorny

[23]Cf. especially Mk 14.65 and Lk 22.64, but also Mt 26.67–68.
[24]This quote has defied my attempts to identify its source.
[25]Ps 44.3.
[26]Is 53.2.
[27]Cf. Is 53.4–5.
[28]Lam 1.12.
[29]This implies, then, that the Church is the true mother (cf. Gal 4.26).

spines they pricked his holy head so much that they penetrated to the brain, [and] they caused unspeakable pain to the unmalicious Lamb of God, our Savior and Redeemer. Considering all of this with your mind, God-loving soul, be terrified and, falling to the earth with trembling, with tears say the prayer, "Our Father." And a bow.

Holy godly contemplation, let us go again after Christ on his way; for, when the evil tormenters seized Jesus, they commanded him, and he went forth bearing his cross, on which he wished to be crucified.[30] This cross was very heavy, for, as some doctors[31] of the church say, it was fifty feet in length, that is, fifty paces. And this then was the heaviness the Son of God bore on his shoulders. Consider how great his pain must have been when his wounds were caused to ripped open anew, chafed by such heaviness of the wood of the cross. But even so they set upon him, striking and shoving. They tormented him so much that he could bear no more, and he fell on the way. Then they ordered Simon of Cyrene to bear his cross to the mount of Golgotha, where he was to be.[32] So you, right-believing soul, going after your teacher, unite yourself to his mother, the most blessed Virgin Mary, going after Jesus with the other women, weeping and lamenting. Do you yourself weep and lament also. Rend your hardened and stony heart, so that the Son of God, going to the voluntary Passion, may comfort even you, so that he may say even to you, as to those who followed him, "Daughters of Jerusalem, do not weep over me, but over yourselves and your children."[33] O our delightful comfort, Christ our Savior, make us worthy joyfully to behold you when you come with your glory to judge the living and the dead. Then receive even us, who call to mind your holy sufferings, into your kingdom, and make us worthy joyfully to delight in sight of your countenance[34] unto unending ages. And so saying this, or meditating, say the prayer, "Our Father." And a bow.

[30]Cf. Jn 19:17.
[31]I have not been able to identify the "doctors" of whom St Dimitri speaks here.
[32]Cf. Mk 15.21, Mt 27.32, Lk 23.26.
[33]Lk 23.28.
[34]Cf. Ps 4.7.

Moreover, holy godly contemplation, recall how it was for him, our Savior, when they nailed his most pure hands and feet to the cross with long, sharp, iron nails, with the greatest violence; what sort of pain he endured then, and how much of his blood was shed. Then, I think, he shed it for us all the way down to the last drop. So this is how they raised him on the cross. Then it was possible to number all his bones, just as the prophet David says in his person: "They numbered all my bones."[35] Certain doctors[36] of the church consider three of Christ's pains to be the gravest. The first is when they stretched him on the cross so violently that all his members opened up and it was possible to number them. The second is when, during these most violent sufferings of his, he saw many who were ungrateful for his good deed, and unbelieving. On this account he was violently pained at heart and prayed to God, his Father, as the apostle said: "In the days of his flesh, with a powerful cry and with tears, he brought prayers and supplications to the one who could save him from death, and he was heard because of his piety."[37] The third pain was when our Savior was extremely crushed in his heart when he saw his Mother standing before the cross, wounded with sorrow and pain in her heart, as with a sword, in accordance with what was said to her by Simeon: "And a sword shall pierce your own heart also."[38]

When our Savior saw her then, as if dead from sorrow, lamenting, in pain, and calling out to him with tears, "O my Son, how do you endure this violent and dishonorable death? I cannot endure seeing you suffering so!"—when our Savior heard this and saw her suffering very violently in her maternal heart and devoured by sorrow, he was pained in his heart. Certain doctors[39] speak of this in

[35]Ps 21:18.

[36]Once again, these "doctors" have escaped my identification.

[37]Heb 5.7.

[38]Cf. Lk 2.35. St Dimitri substitutes the word "heart" for the scriptural "soul," suggesting, if only vaguely, a possible devotion to Mary's heart parallel to or inspired by Latin devotion to the (Immaculate, or Holy) Heart of Mary.

[39]This idea has a long history in the Roman Catholic Church. See the discussion in Alphonsus de Liguori, *The Glories of Mary* (New York: P. J. Kennedy & Sons, 1888),

this way, and testify that if it were possible to gather into one the sufferings of all the martyrs who suffered for Christ, however much they be, and, gathering together all of these, to compare them with the suffering of the most pure Virgin Mary, yet she suffered more than all, even if not in body, but rather in soul, co-suffering guilt-lessly with her suffering Son and God. Reading about these things, or meditating, say to the Theotokos, "Rejoice, Virgin Theotokos."[40] And a bow.

Holy godly contemplation, do you not wish to be present before our crucified Savior on the cross and hear his final, most sweet words, which he spoke on the cross, which are seven in number?

O sweetest Lamb Jesus Christ!

O Sladchaishij Agnche Iisuse Khriste! [O Sweetest Lamb Jesus Christ!]. Illustration from St Dimitri of Rostov, *Sochinenija* [Works], vol. 1 (Moscow: Sinodal'naja Tipografija, 1839), 254.

515ff. Alphonus was active a generation after St Dimitri, but he provides the testimony of many earlier writers.

[40]See above, p. 75, footnote 13.

The Words of Christ Spoken on the Cross

First

Praying for those carrying out the crucifixion, he said this to his Father: "Father, forgive them, for they do not know what they do."[41]

Considering this, God-loving man, do you also forgive your enemies their transgressions, and pray for them, that their transgressions be forgiven. Then do you yourself ask forgiveness of God with tenderness and tears, and say: "I have sinned, forgive me!"

Second

When some passing by blasphemed him, wagging their heads, they said, "Lo! You who destroy the church[42] and in three days raise it up, save yourself; if you are the Son of God, come down from the cross."[43] Then the thieves who were crucified with him abused him also. Jesus, hearing these things, how abuse from the ungrateful nation sorrowed him even on the cross with their ingratitude, and how his enemies abused him all day long, cried out in a loud voice, saying, "My God, my God! Why have you forsaken me?"[44]

Recalling these word of Christ, cry out to him with great tenderness of heart; cry out to him, crying to God the Father and also to God the Holy Spirit: "God the Son, Word of God, Christ my Savior, suffering for my sake on the cross in the flesh, hear me crying out to you, 'My God, why have you forsaken me?' Lift up the one who is fallen, vivify the one mortified by a multitude of sins, lest I perish in sins, but rather receive my repentance and have mercy as the lover of mankind."

[41]Lk 23.34.
[42]See above, p. 57, footnote 4.
[43]Mt 27.40, Mk 15.29.
[44]Mt 27.46.

Third

One of the evildoers hanging with him blasphemed him, saying, "If you are the Christ, save yourself and us."[45] But the other answered, preventing him, saying, "Do you not fear God, when you yourself are condemned to the same? For we are condemned rightfully, since we have received what befits our deeds, but he has done not one evil thing." And he said to Jesus, "Remember me, Lord, when you come in your kingdom." And Jesus said to him, "Amen, I say to you, today you shall be with me in paradise."[46]

Meditating on this merciful word of Christ to the penitent thief, let us also approach him with fervent repentance, confessing our sins, just as the thief of good understanding did not hide his sins, but rather confessed that it was according to his desserts that he suffered for his sins, and simultaneously confessed the innocence of the Son of God, and believed he was not a simple man, but the Lord, and he let out this cry to him, believing him to be King and Lord, true God. And this execution that was carried out upon [the thief of good understanding] was accounted to him [as suffering] for his sins, and he departed, in accordance with the word of the Lord, into his kingdom. And therefore let us also cry out to him, repenting just like the thief: "Remember me, Lord, when you come in your kingdom."[47]

Fourth

Jesus, seeing his Mother and the disciple whom he loved standing before the cross, said to his Mother, "Woman, behold your son." And then he said to his disciple, "Behold your mother."[48]

[45] Lk 23.39.
[46] Lk 23.40–43.
[47] Lk 23.42.
[48] Jn 19.27.

A sermon of St John Chrysostom on the crucifixion of the Lord, concerning the lamentation of the most holy Theotokos.[49]

"Why did the Mother, who bore the most pure one, suffer unendurably? For what reason? Because she is a mother. What pities did not wound her soul? Which arrows did not pierce her inner parts? Which lances did not tear at her being? Therefore she could not contain herself together with [her] companions standing with her around the cross, co-afflicted and weeping with her over the misfortune—she could not stand even a little distant. Not having the strength to endure the shuddering of heart and wishing to hear the last words of her beloved Son, she came forward and, standing before the cross and lamenting, she cried out, 'What is this strange sight, unendurable to my eyes, Master? What is this wonder that darkens every thought and the very brightness of the sun, O my Son? What is this inconceivable mystery, sweet Jesus? I cannot endure seeing you naked who are clothed with light as with a garment![50] And now what do I see? For your garment the soldiers cast lots—for the garment that I wove with my own hands. I am torn in my inner parts, seeing you hanging in the midst of the whole universe on a high tree in between two evildoers. You lead one into paradise, revealing an image of the conversion of the nations, and you suffer long the other who blasphemes, who possesses an image of Jewish cruelty. O envy! You have passed over all the righteous who have lived from the age and have touched my sweetest child! O supermundane and bodiless powers! Come together with me and lament. O sun! Have compassion on my child, change into darkness, for already the light of my eyes shall quickly pass away under the earth. O moon! Hide your beams, for already the ray of my soul enters into the tomb. Where has your comeliness been hid, you who are the most exceedingly beautiful of all the sons of men?[51] How has the brightness of your eyes darkened, eye that dries the deeps?' Saying this, the Theotokos

---

[49]I have been unable to identify the source of this quotation.
[50]Ps 103.2.
[51]Ps 44.3.

was spent, and, standing before the cross, covering her face with her hands, she was exhausted in despair. So Jesus, bowing his head to the right side and quietly opening his mouth, declared, 'Woman! Behold your Son,' indicating his disciple, John the Theologian." Meditating on all of this, right-believing soul, with tears pray to God, saying, "Lord, have mercy!"

Fifth

After this, Jesus, knowing that all was finished, said, so that the scripture might be fulfilled, "I thirst."[52] A vessel full of vinegar stood nearby. Filling a sponge with vinegar, theyput it on a reed and raised it to his mouth. Recalling this, with tenderness of heart let us cry out to him: "You who are crucified for us, Christ our Savior, our sweetness, give us a drink of sweetness to drink from the abundance of your house, and when you come with glory to judge, let us be satisfied when your glory is manifest. And do not despise us here, who hunger and thirst, but grant us to be worthy communicants of the most pure mysteries of your body and blood, which you have poured out for us—make us worthy, and show us to be uncondemned unto ages of ages."

Sixth

When Jesus had received the vinegar, he said, "It is finished!"[53] Recalling this word, say: "Christ, our Savior and Redeemer, show us perfect[54] before you unto the ages, so that, walking the path of your commandments, we may be revealed perfect[55] in good deeds and

[52]Jn 19.28.

[53]Jn 19.30.

[54]There is a pun here. In Slavonic, "It is finished" is *sovershaetsja*, and "perfect" is *sovershennyj*, the passive participial form of the perfective of this same verb. My thanks to Fr Ignatius Green, who suspected, on the basis of Greek, that such a play on words might be present here (in Greek, "it is finished" [*tetelestai*] and the word "perfect" [*telos*] are also related).

[55]See footnote immediately above.

hear that most-desired voice: 'Come, blessed of my Father, inherit the kingdom prepared for you.'"[56]

Seventh

Crying out with a great voice, Jesus said, "Father! Into your hands I commend my spirit."[57] Saying this, and so bowing his head, he gave up the spirit.[58] Here, godly contemplation, stand in meditation: Who commended the spirit? The Son of God, our Creator and our Redeemer. Therefore, with great desire of heart, speak to him in this way: "When the dread hour of the separation of my soul from the body comes, then, my Redeemer, receive it into your hands and keep it free from all afflictions, lest my soul behold the dark gaze of the wicked demons; but rather may it pass saved through all the tollhouses, O our Savior. We faithfully hope to receive this from your love for mankind and loving-kindness." Inasmuch as it was Friday, and lest the bodies remain on the cross on Saturday, since that Saturday was a great day, the Jews prayed Pilate that they break their knees and take them down. So the soldiers came and broke the knees of the first and of the other one crucified with him. But coming to Jesus, they saw that he was already dead, [and] his knees they did not break. But one of the soldiers pierced his side with a lance, and at once there came forth blood and water:[59] blood for our sanctification, and water for washing. Then the whole creation was changed with fear, beholding the life of all hanging dead on the tree. And Joseph of Arimathea came, requested the body of Jesus and, taking it down from the tree, he laid it in his own new tomb. Arise, Lord our God, and deliver us for your name's sake![60] Amen.

[56]Mt 25.34.
[57]Lk 23.46.
[58]Jn 19.30.
[59]Jn 19.31–34.
[60]Ps 48.27.

10

A Thankful Recollection of the Sufferings of Christ and a Prayerful Meditation, More Useful than All Other Prayers, Which Should Be Performed on All Fridays

This beginning:

"Blessed is our God . . . ," *but if a monk or layperson, then,* "Through the prayers of our holy fathers. . . ." *Then,* "Glory to you, our God, glory to you . . . ," "O Heavenly King . . . ," *Trisagion. After* "Our Father," "Lord, have mercy," 12 times. "Glory . . . both now. . . ." "Come let us worship," *thrice.*[1] "Have mercy on me, O God. . . ."[2] "I believe in one God, the Father. . . ."[3]

After this, say these verses:

[1.] O how sweet and how beautiful is your coming, O Son of God, come down from heaven! For while seeking the lost sheep,[4] the man who had sinned, you undertook many innumerable labors, many travels, and after these, you went to the Passion and voluntary death,

---

[1]"Blessed is our God . . ." through "Come let us worship . . ." is the "typical beginning" of most Orthodox prayer services, both in the church and "in the cell" (that is, in private).

[2]The incipit of Ps 50.

[3]See above, p. 75, footnote 9.

[4]Cf. Lk 15.1–7.

for which, my Creator and Redeemer, I send up thanksgiving to you from my whole heart!

At each verse, make a bow.

[2.] You, the second Adam, who were taken and strongly bound in the garden of Gethsemane on behalf of the first Adam, who sinned in paradise—[O] Jesus Christ, Son of God, glory to you, glory to you! Bind me with your love so strongly that I would rather choose death than sometime to offend your lack of malice and love for mankind by some sin, I pray to you.

[3.] Led from the garden through the Kidron valley, thrown down on the way and fallen to the earth, Lord Jesus Christ, glory to you, glory to you! I fall down before you, at your most pure feet: from every fall of my soul, guard me, I pray to you.

[4.] You are led from Annas to the wretched high priest Caiaphas, where you suffered beatings upon your most pure cheeks, which are beautiful, like a garden of sweet-smelling fragrances.[5] Glory to you, glory to you, Lord Jesus Christ, Son of God, glory to you!

[5.] And so, in this way, before Caiaphas you were slapped on the cheek with an iron, armed hand by the ungrateful Malchus—whose ear, cut off by Peter in the garden, you healed[6]—so hard, Lord, that all the fingers of that cursed hand are brought together on your most holy face; your teeth, whiter than milk,[7] are tried; your slapping is heard throughout the whole of the high-priestly palace. You fell at once to the earth, [and] from your most pure mouth, and also from your nose, you poured out[8] much divine blood, O spring[9] of our life; Lord Jesus Christ, Son of God, I sing to you: glory to you, glory to you!

[5]Cf. Song 5.13.

[6]Cf. Jn 18.10–11 and also Mt 26.51, Mk 14.47, and Lk 22.50–51.

[7]Cf. Gen 49.12; cf. also Song 4.2 and 6.6, though these latter are seemingly addressed to the bride and not the bridegroom.

[8]*Istochil.*

[9]*Istochnik.*

[6.] Before that same Caiaphas, the lying and lie-loving high priest, when you heard lying testimonies against you, you were nonetheless like a dumb lamb, opening not your mouth,[10] but rather silently enduring all: Lord Jesus Christ, Son of God, glory to you, glory to you! Grant me silence and patience toward those who oppose me with fervor, rising up against me on account of whomever, lest lying and a lie be found in my mouth, I pray to you.

[7.] When your most holy face was covered in abuse, and you were slapped on the face, then were you asked, "Who is it slapping you?"[11] Lord Jesus Christ, Son of God, glory to you! Cover my sins with forgiveness, lest eternal shame cover my face when I shall stand before your face; make me worthy to behold it and be satisfied, I pray to you.

[8.] By the senseless gathering of the Jews and by Caiaphas, since you were called a blasphemer and a transgressor of the law, you were said to be condemned to death, [and] deep into the night you were abused and humiliated by the Jews, slapped many times in the high-priestly palace, and also thrown into a dungeon until morning: Lord Jesus Christ, glory to you, glory to you, unsetting light! After my departure from this life free my soul from the dungeon of Gehenna, I pray to you.

[9.] When morning had come, you were bound by the Jews and led to Pontius Pilate the governor, who found not one thing worthy of condemnation in you, you who are guilty of our salvation: Lord Jesus Christ, Son of God, glory to you! Therefore keep me throughout my whole life, lest, at the hour of my death, the enemy, the opponent of my soul, find one thing worthy of condemnation in me, I pray to you.

[10.] You were led from Pilate to the city, to the foolish Herod, who had long desired to see you, although he was foolish and indifferent,

[10]Cf. Is 53.7.
[11]Cf. Mt 26.67–68, Mk 14.65, and Lk 22.64.

considering you, the uncreated Wisdom from before the ages, to be without sense, [and] he humiliated you, and when he had abused you, [he] covered you in a bright garment: glory to you, Lord Jesus Christ, my God, glory to you! Guard me from the abuse of unseen enemies and cover me in a garment of incorruption after my death, I pray to you!

[11.] Herod again returned you, disgraced, to the cowardly Pilate, and you were led to him, suffering many blows and offenses for my sake on that path: glory to you, Lord Jesus Christ, my God, glory to you! Direct my paths toward the light of your commandments, I pray to you.

[12.] From Pilate you were led out and led to the pillar, where, taking off your own garment from yourself, and embracing the pillar of your own will, you, guiltless in hands and pure in heart, fixed your most holy hands in bondage to the pillar, desiring to loose and free human nature from the hands of the enemy! So by the hands of the fierce soldiers you were very strongly tied and bound to the pillar, beaten so unmercifully with cold, thorny branches, with sharply knotted cords, and with hooked iron fetters, and, standing at the pillar, you received blows across your most holy body, and after these sores you were again beaten fiercely, [and] you endured wounds such that your divine body hung beaten off the bones, just like black swellings; and your life-creating blood flowed out most abundantly. So, loosed from the pillar and very weakened by pain, you fell to the ground and lying on the ground in your own blood, according to nature you were required to die from such wounds and pains; but your divinity shall remain passionless, granting being to all creation. Glory to you, Lord Jesus Christ, my God, glory to you! For the sake of these priceless and all-healing sores of yours, forgive all my sins and keep me from the wounding of the enemy even unto the end, I pray to you.

[13.] After such sores and tortures, you were all naked, clothed only with your blood. You are naked, just as at your birth; you are abused with great coldness, [and] before all your garments are taken away from you one by one: you who were only just barely clinging to life, and shaking from pain and frost, for it was winter,[12] you who created sun and fire for the warming of those born on earth, Lord Jesus Christ, Son of God, glory to you, glory to you! Warm my cold heart unto virtue with the warmth of your Most Holy Spirit, who came down in fire,[13] I pray to you.

[14.] O death-bearing pillar of stone, O earth struck to death: glory to you, Lord Jesus Christ, Son of God, glory to you! Be for me a pillar of might against the face of the enemy, I pray to you.

[15.] Kicked with feet, torn and dragged by the hair and by the beard, Lord Jesus Christ, Son of God, glory to you, glory to you! Lest my soul be seized by the teeth of the serpent of Gehenna, keep [it] in your blood, I pray to you.

[16.] By the filthy hands of the deicide Jewish race you are struck at the legs and knees with weapons and clubs even until you stumble. You, who are the King exalted above heaven and earth, who were lifted up from the ground by your hair and ears, which were upon your most holy neck, Lord Jesus Christ, Son of God, I call out to you: glory to you, glory to you, glory to you! Hang up and raise up my mind, so that I may ever consider heavenly things and act with the compassion of your love for mankind, for whose sake you suffer.

[17.] From the crown of thorns you endured thousands of punctures, then you poured out divine and priceless drops of blood from your head. The crown of thorns was lifted up and laid down on your most pure head, [O] most beautiful head of the Church! Glory to you, Lord Jesus Christ, Son of God, glory to you!

[12]Cf. Jn 10.22.
[13]Cf. Acts 2.3–4.

[18.] After the crown of thorns you were beaten on the head with reeds and shields with all their might, and therefore they pierced your pure and most holy head most deeply with the points of the thorns, and by their efforts the points pierced deep into your brain. I am pierced deeply by the sharp thorns of soul-fighting passions, therefore I call out to you: glory to you, Lord Jesus Christ, Son of God, glory to you!

[19.] You who, as an insult from the Jews, received the reed given into your right hand, as to a king,[14] you who sit at the right hand of the God and Father,[15] Lord Jesus Christ, Son of God, glory to you, glory to you! With this reed set aright the handwriting of my numerous transgressions,[16] that I may stand at your right hand in your glory and glorify you unto the ages.

[20.] Lord, you who are struck with fists across your divine body, on your mouth, and between your eyes, you whose eyes are like a fiery flame, and who are struck on your most holy neck: bow my neck, I pray you; make me mighty in worship of you, who for our sake bowed the heavens and came down.[17] Lord Jesus Christ, Son of God, glory to you, glory to you; do not drive me away from your heavenly glory.

[21.] You who accepted striking on the head and breast, accept even the bowing of my head and fervent beating of the breast, just as you once accepted the publican's;[18] make me mighty with your most holy right hand, so that I may thankfully bear striking, and every sorrow and temporary burden; for all things whatsoever that you wish, you arrange for the good. Glory to you, Lord Jesus Christ, Son of God, glory to you; make me worthy of your divine glory, I pray to you.

[14]Cf. Mt 27.29.
[15]Cf. Heb 10.12.
[16]The image is that of a pen being used to rewrite a bill of debt.
[17]Cf. Ps 17.10 (also 2 Sam 22.10).
[18]*Mytarstvo*, literally, "tax collection" or "tollbooth," though the reference to the striking of the breast makes it clear that the reference is to the Lucan parable (Lk 18.9–14).

[22.] You were torn and ferociously wounded on the nose and on the ears with abuse and severe torture, [and] have no wholeness from foot to head, nor an image of comeliness, [and] bearing a crown of thorns, clothed in a crimson garment of abuse, you were led a second time before Pilate, who, when he saw you in incurable sores and pains, wondered so much at the inhuman ferocity of the Jews that he said concerning you, "Has not this man been beaten so mercilessly that he is worthy of some good will from the Jews? But they called out to him, 'Crucify him!'"[19] But I call out to you, Word of God: glory to you, Lord Jesus Christ, Son of God, glory to you! Uproot the thorn of sins from the earth of my stony heart, so that I may bring forth for you the fruit of thanksgiving.

[23.] You who bring forth water from a rock[20] and wind from your treasuries,[21] you were led to the senseless Pilate, who set you in the place of judgment and condemned you, who sit on the cherubim[22] and judge the living and the dead,[23] who are guiltless, to death. Glory to you, Lord Jesus Christ, Son of God, glory to you, my God; grant me always the remembrance of death, and to be ready for your dread and righteous judgment, at which judge me not according to my deeds, but save me according to your mercy, I pray to you.

[24.] When Pilate announced the sentence of death spoken against you, the giver of ineffable life, then the Jews, bound by a lack of good disposition, bound your hands and laid the cross on your most holy neck, and led you out to death between two thieves, like an evildoer. You who are numbered[24] with the lawless, unchanging[25] Lord Jesus Christ, Son of God, glory to you; from the evil activity of the invisible thief, who undermines the building of my soul with various

[19]Lk 23.21.
[20]Cf. Ex 17.6, Num 20.11, etc.
[21]Cf. Jer 10.13, Ps 134.7.
[22]A common biblical image: cf., e.g., 1 Sam 4.4, 2 Sam 6.2, Is 37.16.
[23]Cf. 2 Tim 4.1, 1 Pet 4.5.
[24]*Vmenennyj.* (Cf. Mk 15.28, Lk 22.37, both quoting Is 53.12.)
[25]*Neizmennyj.*

temptations, keep me day and night as the apple of your eye,[26] lest I be robbed of the treasure of eternal blessings that you have prepared for those who love you,[27] I pray to you.

[25.] [And] still, [O] depth of mercy, the unmerciful Jewish race laid upon you a very heavy cross, bearing which on your own, you fell to the ground, and then received deadly blows. Well-disposed Lord Jesus Christ, Son of God, glory to you, glory to you! For the sake of these your wonders, by the cross keep me from the fall of the enemy, I pray to you.

[26.] You were led out to the mount of Golgotha, Master of powers and authorities on high, yourself voluntarily deprived of your garments, [and] you suffered pain. For when your robe was taken, then all your sores opened up and, tearing [at you], they renewed your pain, you who renewed human nature, [and] I pray to you: peeling away from my soul the ancient scabs of the lawless passions that cling to it, receive me, who call out: ineffable in your suffering, Lord Jesus Christ, Son of God, glory to you, glory to you, long-suffering Master!

[27.] You who, by spitting, once gave light for seeing to the man blind from birth,[28] who were dishonored by the Jews by filthy spitting across your most bright face before the crucifixion, who are more honorable than all ranks of angels, Lord Jesus Christ, Son of God, glory to you, glory to you; make me mighty in the face of constant filthiness and in the face of the spitting of the enemy's snares, temptations, and fleshly delights, I pray to you.

[28.] When the violent Jewish people led you out to Golgotha, they set the cross on the ground, so that upon it they might crucify you, who stretch out heaven like a tent,[29] and at the same time you yourself immutably desired to be placed on the cross. But directing

[26]Cf. Ps 16.8.
[27]Cf. 1 Cor 2.9.
[28]Cf. Jn 9.1–7.
[29]Ps 103.2.

tortures of bestial kind against you with one soul, they pounded you onto the cross, and so unmercifully did they nail your most holy hands and feet to the cross with the holy nails that your tendons and joints were all ripped. And then what was said concerning you by the prophet David came to pass: "They numbered all my bones."[30] That pain was most violent, and heavier for you than all your [previous] sufferings; by it heal all the pain of my soul, I pray to you and call out: glory to you, glory to you, Lord Jesus Christ, Son of God; for the sake of your most glorious, most pure, and life-creating sufferings, save me, Master, great in mercy and lover of mankind!

[29.] Cleansing the lepers, most pure one, more beautiful with comeliness than all the sons of men,[31] you are yourself become as a leper by filthy defilement with spit, which, while stretched on the cross lying on the ground, you received on various parts of your divine body. Glory to you, Lord Jesus Christ, my God, glory to you! Cleanse my leprous soul from indescribable sinful defilements and save me, I pray to you.

[30.] You who let out heartfelt sighs before your death on the cross, pouring out drops of tears during your life-creating Passion, and also drops of blood, pour out on me your loving-kindness and grant me heartfelt sighs over my sins; give me tears that cleanse away sin, and moreover cleanse and wash my soul with your most pure blood and tears, so that I may sing: glory to you, Lord Jesus Christ, my God, who suffered all these things for my sake, glory to you!

[31.] You who on the cross are raised all naked, having only your waist covered with a small covering, hung between two thieves, fed with gall and vinegar, my most sweet Jesus, glory to you, glory to you! From the bitterness of sin and the deceits of the enemy keep me, I pray to you.

---

[30]Ps 21.18.
[31]Cf. Ps 44.3.

[32.] Creator of my soul and body, who suffered for my sake across your whole body, with all your soul and senses: with the sense of touch, the beating and wounding of your whole flesh; with the sense of taste, drinking the gall and vinegar; with the sense of smell, the burden of the stench at the repository of corpses on the mount of Golgotha;[32] with the sense of hearing, lying testimonies, abuses, and blasphemies; with the sense of sight, the flowing of bitter tears and painful sight of your most pure Mother standing under the cross and violently rending her own heart. Glory to you, Lord Jesus Christ, my God, glory to you; forgive me, a wretch, all the ways I have sinned with my senses of soul and body, for the sake of your honorable saving suffering.

[33.] Spring of immortality, who died at the ninth hour,[33] grant me, after my death, to live where the nine ranks[34] of angels praise and hymn you, I now pray to you; by the power of all your travels, deeds, and labors, which for our sake you undertook while living on the earth little more than three and thirty years, timeless One of the Trinity, Lord Jesus Christ, receive from me, unworthy and filthy, a thirty and thrice recollection of your most pure sufferings as an immaculate sacrifice, since I have remembered your sacrifice which you offered on the altar of the cross and the whole world; remember the prayers offered for us by your all-holy Virgin Mother and your beloved friend and disciple John the Theologian, and the holy equal-to-the-apostles Mary Magdalene, and the others who stand before your cross offering prayers to you on our behalf. For you are the truth, and truly you wish that all be saved,[35] and to you from all belongs glory, honor, praise, and worship, now and ever and unto ages of ages. Amen.

[32]I can find no evidence for a tradition that Golgotha was a "repository of corpses." Perhaps St Dimitri (or a source of his) has confused traditions surrounding Golgotha with those surrounding Gehenna.

[33]Cf. Mt 27.45, Mk 15.33, Lk 23.44.

[34]That there are nine ranks of angels is a commonplace in the Christian tradition.

[35]Cf. 1 Tim 2.4.

The authors, historians, witnesses, and teachers, the ecclesiastical writers on the sufferings of the Lord, are these: St Athanasius the Great, St Eusebius of Samosata, St John Chrysostom, St Cyprian, St Epiphanius of Cyprus, St John of the Ladder, St Ambrose of Milan, St Theodoret,[36] St Jerome,[37] St John Damascene, St Leo the Pope of Rome, St John of the Ladder, St Isidore of Pelusium, and other saints.

This prayerful meditation on the Lord's sufferings was composed by the effort and labors of the Most Reverend Dimitri, Metropolitan of Rostov and Yaroslavl, in the year of the incarnation of God the Word 1702.

---

[36]Later Russian tradition knows Theodoret of Cyrrhus as "Blessed Theodoret,"—see for example the book of N. N. Glubokovskij, *Blazhennyj Feodorit, episkop Kirrskij: ego zhizn' i literaturnaja dejatel'nost'* [Blessed Theodoret, Bishop of Cyrrhus: His Life and Literary Activity], 2 vols. (Moscow: Universitetskaja tipografija, 1890), later republished electronically (Moscow: Perervinskaja dukhovnaja seminarija, 2005), especially the discussion in vol. 1, ch. 7, esp. 347ff. and most especially the poem in honor of Theodoret by St John of Euchaita, 348—but I know of nowhere else in the Orthodox tradition where Theodoret is explicitly called a saint; perhaps this title comes from Latin sources, or perhaps St Dimitri has confused Theodoret with St Theodoret of Antioch, a martyr commemorated on October 23rd. This latter saint is not included in St Dimitri's *Lives* but is in modern Russian calendars.

[37]St Dimitri's reliance on St Jerome's works and teachings in his *Lives of the Saints* was one of the two "heresies" of which Patriarch Joachim (in a 1689 letter) accused him upon the publication of the first volume, the other being St Dimitri's belief that "the Most Holy Theotokos was conceived and born without original sin." According to Joachim, "the holy Church does not number [Jerome] in the catalog of saints and does not accept his teachings" (quoted in Fedotova, *Epistoljarnoe nasledie* [Epistolary Legacy], 49; trans. present author). For more, see the introduction to the present volume, p. 16.

11

Lamentation for the Burial of Christ

Where are you going, borne away, sweetest Jesus? Where are you going from us, our hope and refuge? Where are you hiding from our eyes, our light, never-setting sun? How shall you know your setting?[1]

Stop, you who bear him who bears the whole world in his palm! Stop, you who bear him who has borne the burden of the sin of the whole human race! You who bear him, stop, seeing on the cross him by whom the sun and the moon are set in their order.

Do not forbid us children[2] to come to our father,[3] though he is already dead. Do not forbid his children[4] to lament over the common parent of all, who bore us by his blood! Grant them to pour out at least a small teardrop from their eyes over the one who poured out rich floods of his blood for us from his whole body, and water and blood from his side.

O what is this I see? A dread, terrible vision! O what is this I see? I see something that the eyes of the forefathers never saw from the beginning of the ages. For who ever saw God stripped naked, beaten, crowned with thorns, given gall and vinegar to drink, wounded with nails and a lance, and killed? The heavens are afraid, terrified at this, and may the foundations of the earth be shaken.[5]

---

[1] These lines recall the service read at compline on Holy Friday. Cf. esp. ode 4, troparion 1 of the canon, and also the ikos.

[2] *Detjam.*

[3] "Father" is an unusual title for Christ, but clearly scriptural (Is 9.6).

[4] *Chadam.*

[5] Jer 2.12.

What is this I see? I see God without breath, the life-giver dead, light darkened, sweetness embittered. The one exceedingly more beautiful with comeliness than all the sons of men[6] I see having neither appearance nor comeliness;[7] rather his appearance is dishonored and belittled above all the sons of men.[8]

I see the most pure, most blessed body of my Christ—ineffably born from the most pure, most blessed Virgin—bloodied, all wounded, torn like sackcloth, having no wholeness from the feet to the head.[9]

The wounded head most pure, the head which arranges everything by its wisdom, directs all, and uncovers wondrous means for the salvation of despairing man—this head is wounded unto the brain by sharp thorny spines. Now we see the Word of God fallen among thorns, which, growing up, have choked him.[10] Now we see the fulfillment of the ancient words of God to man, when he said, "Cursed is the earth in your deeds, thorns and thistles shall it sprout forth for you."[11] Behold, the wretched earth has sprouted up thorns for the head of my Jesus!

The eyes are darkened, those eyes which have looked down upon all with loving-kindness [and] gazed upon all with love; eyes in whose bright glance those who love him have rejoiced, those who are sorrowful have been comforted, and those who are sinful have turned to repentance: these [eyes] have streamed with tears and blood and been confronted with dying.

Darkened is the face, the face most honorable, most bright, angelic in appearance, or rather God-like in appearance, which, when it was made to shine on Tabor by the glory of divinity, shone like the sun; this face is now spat upon, dishonored, slapped with a

[6]Ps 44.3.
[7]Is 53.2.
[8]Is 53.3.
[9]Is 1.6.
[10]Mt 13.7. In Jesus' explanation of the parable, the seed is explicitly called the Word. See Mt 13.19ff.
[11]Gen 13.17–18.

strong hand, filled with bruises: your comeliness has disappeared, O most beautiful, O most beloved!

The most sweet mouth, from which flowed a flood of heavenly sweetness, words sweeter than honey and honeycomb,[12] is now fallen silent, made bitter by gall and vinegar. Fallen silent is the God-speaking tongue, fallen silent is the throat of the divine voice; silence has settled upon the Word of God. So who shall comfort those lamenting? Who with a word will heal the sick and raise the dead? Who shall say to the sinful woman, "Her many sins are forgiven"?[13]

Wounded are the hands, the hands at whose touch death trembled, hands which were like a healing bandage for every sickness, hands by which small breads were multiplied to a great abundance for the satisfaction of thousands of the people. These hands are wounded straight through with long, sharp, iron nails, [and are] bruised by being bound: the hands which made man are inhumanly tormented by man.

Wounded are the feet which walked on the waters as on dry land, the feet which the sinful woman washed with her tears and wiped with her hair, [and so] received forgiveness of her many sins;[14] these are the feet which, should someone be made worthy to be a footstool for them,[15] this one would be higher than the whole world. These feet were also pierced straight through with long iron nails so that his foot might be moistened in blood.

The pierced life-bearing side of him who, from the side, made a helper for our forefather Adam; now he, the heavenly bridegroom, makes from his own side his holy Church—a beloved[16] bride for himself and a beloved[17] mother for us—so that she may bear many children by water and the Spirit.[18]

---

[12] Ps 18.11.
[13] Lk 7.47.
[14] Lk 7.36–50.
[15] Cf. Ps 98.5, and also Is 66.1.
[16] *Vozljubennuju.*
[17] *Ljubeznuju.*
[18] Cf. Jn 3.5.

Our Lord has called himself a door, saying, "I am the door: if someone shall enter by me, he shall be saved."[19] And again he said: "Knock, and it shall be opened to you."[20] But now there is no need to knock at [this door], for a soldier's hand has knocked at it with a lance and opened it wide: "One of the soldiers pierced his side with a lance."[21] Behold, therefore, this door is open: each one who wishes, let him enter therein, and "go out and find pasture."[22]

Pierced is the side with a long, sharp, iron lance, which, going through the inner parts [by virtue of] its length, reached the very heart and wounded it. It wounded the heart that was the spring and beginning of all love; it wounded the heart that loved its own who are in the world, unto the end it loved them;[23] it wounded the heart pained at heart, loving-kind, compassionate toward the afflicted. The world wounded the heart of Christ because Christ loved the world with all his heart. Now we know how Christ loves the ungrateful world: God so loved the world, that he spared not his own heart for its sake.[24]

Fiercely blazing was the heart of Christ, blazing measurelessly with hot love for man, and so as to be cooled a bit from this heat, he willed to receive cold iron inside his heart, so that a cool wind might pass over the warmth of his heart. The side opened like a door in order to receive a wound in the heart, like a little open window. Rise up therefore, north wind, and come, south wind, and blow into the heart of our lover, who burns to death with measureless love for us.[25]

Scripture called Christ God a fire, saying, "Our God is a consuming fire,"[26] because, just as he illumines all, so likewise he warms all, and nothing shall be hidden from his warmth.[27] This fire, inasmuch

[19]Jn 10.9.
[20]Mt 7.7.
[21]Jn 19.34.
[22]Jn 10.10.
[23]Jn 3.1.
[24]Jn 3.16, with the word "heart" (*serdtse*) inserted.
[25]Cf. Song 4.16.
[26]Heb 12.29.
[27]Ps 18.7.

as it is strongly inflamed with love toward the human race, is cooled by its very own springs, blood and water, flowing from the side.

Moses once struck a rock with a rod in the desert and waters flowed out. A soldier smote the flank of the rock, Christ, with a lance, and at once there flowed out blood and water.[28] O hand of the torturer, which dared to touch the side of Christ in torture! O rocky hearts which decided on this murder! But the time shall come when they shall look upon him whom they have pierced.[29]

Our Lord poured out two springs from his most pure side, blood and water: water for our washing, blood for our sanctification; water for quenching our thirst, blood for our healing. You who thirst, come to the water;[30] you who are sick in body and soul, approach the healing blood of the immaculate Lamb of God: not by his glory, but by his wounds have we been healed.[31]

Who are those people who sucked honey from a rock?[32] We, O our most precious stone, Christ![33] We suck sweetness from your most pure side. O sweetness, sweetness! With insatiable desire, we wish to be sated by it always! O sweetness, sweetness! With love exceedingly loving, we long to enjoy it forever. You are all desire, all sweetness, Word of God, Son of the Virgin.[34]

You are our father,[35] for, by your death, you have borne us unto life. You are our mother[36] inasmuch as you feed us with your love. So we are your children, suckling your blood like milk from your most pure wounds, as from nipples. O sweetness, sweetness most exceedingly longed for! O sweetness, most exceedingly beloved sweetness!

[28] Jn 19.34.
[29] Zech 12.10, and also Jn 19.37.
[30] Is 55.1.
[31] Is 53.5, and also 1 Pet 2.24.
[32] Deut 32.13.
[33] Or, rock, but in English we say "precious stone."
[34] Cf. Song 5.16.
[35] See above, p. 103, footnote 3.
[36] An uncommon, but basically scriptural, image. Cf. Mt 23.37 and Lk 13.34.

Our eyes do not wish to turn away to another place, away from the sight of your most beloved wounds [which you endured] for us; neither do our mouths desire to stoop somewhere, away from the kissing of your most sweet wounds [which you endured] for us; neither do our hearts desire to cleave to anything else, apart from you. If someone loves something else, let him love himself, just as he wishes. But for us, it is good to cleave to you, our God.[37] O sweetness, sweetness, not defined by any word! O sweetness, sweetness, not confessed by any tongue!

This wretched world, all lying in evil,[38] is exceedingly filled with bitterness, bitter beyond [that of] Meribah.[39] Our Lord, wishing to sweeten this world, bitter and tasting of wormwood, opened in his side a spring of ineffable sweetness, incomparably surpassing all sensual sweetness.[40] But woe is me! In vain this sweetness is altogether disdained. O world, wretched world! With what do you desire to sweeten your bitterness, if you despise this sweetness?

But I disdain the vain world, I gaze upon myself, I see God before my eyes, calling out to me with his wounds, as with a mouth: "I have loved you: love me.[41] I demand nothing else from you, only love. I seek your love. I was born for your sake; from my youth I was in travail for your sake; I hungered, thirsted, and fasted for your sake; I suffered [and] tasted gall and vinegar for your sake; I was crucified, accepted wounds, and died for your sake. For all of this, I desire to receive nothing else from you, only that you would love me." I love you, Lord, my might! The Lord is my firm foundation and my refuge.[42]

What else shall we love, if not you, our most exceedingly beloved Lord, by whom we wish to be loved unto all ages? With what else

[37]Ps 72.28.
[38]Cf. 1 Jn 5.19.
[39]Cf. Ex 15.23.
[40]Cf. Jer 9.15 and 23.15; cf. also Rev 8.11.
[41]Cf. Jn 15.9, and perhaps also Lk 7.47.
[42]Ps 17.2–3 (also 2 Sam 22.2–3). At the divine liturgy, priests and bishops recite these verses thrice immediately before the Creed.

shall we sweeten our bitterness, if not with you, sweetest Jesus, with whom we hope to be sated sweetly throughout all of life without end? Only do you yourself make dwell in us the love that you desire. Grant that we love you and come to love you. Grant us that we desire you and thirst for you. Kindle us in your love, only-begotten Word of God.

May the nails and lance with which you, Lord, were wounded for the sake of our love, be driven into our hearts, that we may come to love you, Lord. May your wounds teach our hearts to be wounded with love for you, Jesus! May your love capture us in your love, Master! Draw us, and we shall hasten after the fragrance of your myrrh.[43]

So I come following you, together with all, O Love that conquers every desire, Jesus! You [were buried] with your body; with our hearts may we be buried together with you. Let the tomb be a tomb for your most pure body, and so may your most pure wounds be a tomb and burial for our hearts. We know that, on the third day, you shall go forth from the tomb; but may our hearts not leave your most pure wounds until we come to dwell in our tombs. After all, what could be more desirable for our hearts, more beloved, more sweet, than your most pure wounds, which we behold with tearful eyes, lovingly touch with our lips—although we are unworthy—and sweetly kiss with our hearts? Amen.

[43]Song 1.3.

12

The Council and Judgment of the Unbelieving Jews Pronounced against Jesus of Nazareth, the Redeemer of the World

The People to Pilate
If you release him, you are no friend of Caesar's.[1] Crucify, crucify him![2] His blood be on us and on our children![3]

His Wife to Pilate
Have nothing to do with this righteous man, for just now I have suffered much over him in a dream.[4]

Simon the Leper[5]
To which law is the rebel subject?

Achaiah[6]
It is not appropriate for those who do not know his guilt to condemn him to death.

Rabam[7]
But why are laws established? Precisely that they may be kept.

[1] Jn 19.12.
[2] Lk 23.21.
[3] Mt 27.25.
[4] Mt 27.19.
[5] Cf. Mt 26.6 and Mk 14.3; cf. also Lk 7.36ff., esp. v. 40.
[6] *Akhaja.* I could find no sources for this name; it seems to be invented.
[7] *Ravam.* Another seemingly invented name.

Caiaphas[8]

You neither know nor understand anything, for it is better for us that one man die for the people than that the whole nation perish.[9]

Jotham[10]

He speaks blasphemy inasmuch as he calls himself the Son of God.[11] Therefore it befits him to undergo [punishment in accordance with] "his"[12] law.

Samech[13]

Let us do this, lest he oppose us. If he does not obey, let him be executed.

Mesa[14]

If he is righteous, then let us turn to him; if he is unrighteous, then let us drive him from us.

Subat[15]

Not one law punishes someone who is not guilty with death. Indeed, what sin has this man committed?

Rozmothil[16]

Why were laws laid down, if they are not kept?

---

[8]Caiaphas appears in the Gospel of Matthew (Mt 26.57ff.) and also the book of Acts (Acts 4.6) as well as several times in the Gospel of John.

[9]Cf. Jn 11.50.

[10]This name is biblical. Cf. 2 Kg 15.

[11]Cf. Jn 5.18, 19.7.

[12]Here, the character of Jotham seems to employ the word "his" saracastically: since Jesus calls himself God's Son, he should be punished in accordance with God's law, or rather, his own law.

[13]*Samekh*. This is the name for a letter of the Hebrew alphabet, but whether that might be the origin of the name found here is hard to say.

[14]*Mesa*. Yet another seemingly invented name.

[15]*Subat*. This name also seems to be invented.

[16]*Rozmofil*. Another seemingly invented name.

Potifar[17]

This liar stirs up the fatherland and the nation.[18] Therefore it is appropriate to banish him.

Rithal[19]

The law is established for no one other than those who are guilty; let him therefore confess his guilt.

Joseph of Arimathea[20]

Truly it will be a filthy evil, if no one in the whole city protects [this] guiltless man.

Jerich[21]

Maybe he is righteous indeed, but all the same he should die, because with his preaching he stirs up the nation to an uproar.

Teres[22]

It is better to punish him with exile or send him to Caesar.

Ptolemy[23]

Is he righteous or unrighteous—but why do we delay? Why do we not quickly condemn him to death or to banishment?

Jehosaphat[24]

Let him be chained and held in continual fetters.

[17]*Putifar*. This name bears an obvious semblance to the name rendered in English as "Potiphar," but the contemporary Slavonic text has *Pentefrij* for Joseph's master in Gen 39.1 and *Petefria* for Aseneth's father in Gen 41.45. Perhaps this serves as evidence corroborating the immediate Western European derivation of this work (see above, pp. 27–28, footnote 37). Both of these biblical figures (if they are in fact different figures) are named Putiphar in the Vulgate, and maybe a Slavonic translator or adapter did not recognize this Latin name to be the same as Slavonic *Pentefrij/Petefria*. Perhaps such a process might also explain some of the other unusual names in the work.

[18]Cf. Lk 23.5.

[19]*Rifal*. Yet another seemingly invented name.

[20]Cf. Mt 27.57, Mk 15.43, Lk 23.50–51, and Jn 19.38.

[21]*Ierikh*. Another seemingly invented name.

[22]*Teres*. Another seemingly invented name.

[23]A biblical name. Cf., e.g., 1 Macc 1.18.

[24]A biblical name, most prominently that of a righteous king of Judah (cf. 1 Kg 15:24, 22 and 2 Chr 17).

Rathinth[25]

Is he righteous or unrighteous? —but if he has not been found guilty by the laws of the great, it is not appropriate that he suffer this.

Seraiah[26]

Let us uproot him, let us uproot this rebel, born for the destruction of the fatherland.

Diarabiah[27]

Indeed, inasmuch as he deceives the people, may he die by death.[28]

Joram[29]

Why are we going to abandon this man,[30] who is righteous, to be punished with death?

Nicodemus[31]

But does our law condemn someone, neither hearing him nor knowing his guilt?[32]

[Pilate]

In accordance with the decision of this court, let this man,[33] who is found guilty with respect to the laws [requiring the punishment] of death, be crucified as an evildoer after many tortures.

We, Pontius Pilate, the governor of Judea, under the most mighty single rule of Caesar, whose most blessed rule may the Most High

---

[25] *Rafinf.* This is another seemingly invented name.

[26] *Sarej.* A biblical name. It is found in the Slavonic text of 1 Esd 5.5 (this book is called 2 Esdras in the contemporary Slavonic Bible, which shares its corpus of Ezra books with the Vulgate but does not use the same names and numbering) in the adjective form *Sareova*. Though the name Seraiah occurs elsewhere in the English Bible, in the Slavonic text, these names are not the same. For example, in 1 Chr 4.13, the Slavonic form of the name rendered Seraiah in English is *Saraia*, not *Sarej*.

[27] *Diarabij.* Once again, this name appears to be invented.

[28] Cf. Gen 2.17 (LXX).

[29] This is the name of various biblical personages: cf., e.g., 2 Kg 8 and 9.

[30] *Muzha*, "man," a specifically male term, and not *cheloveka*.

[31] Cf. Jn 3.1–21, 19.39–42, and also 7.50–51.

[32] Cf. Jn 7.50–51.

[33] Cf. Jn 19.5.

keep, we, presiding at the trial, have had Jesus of Nazareth brought forward, who in senseless speech preaches himself as the Son of God and leads the Jewish people astray from our most praiseworthy law. Therefore we have condemned him to be crucified on a cross. Go, seize and crucify him!

13

The Address of a Sinner to Magdalene, Weeping at the Feet of Christ[1]

Step away, Magdalene, from the feet of Christ,[2]
And grant me a place. I have great sorrow over my sins.
Your defilements are already cleansed by tears,
And your transgressions are already loosed.
I still wallow in sinful filth,
I wish to seek forgiveness at his feet.
Step away, O woman, from the feet of Christ,
So that even I may turn to his ready mercy.
You have already washed yourself with your voluntary tears,

---

[1]The basic form of this poem is thirteen-syllable isosyllabic lines arranged in rhymed couplets, a type of verse typical of the place and time, though some of the lines here have a few syllables more or less. One of the standard forms that early East Slavic learned syllabic verse adopted from Polish was a 7+6 form, with a fixed caesura, though St Dimitri's observance of the caesura is sometimes not very apparent. One wonders whether irregularities with respect to the number of syllables in a line and possible lapses in the observance of the caesura are a product of the intervention of copyists and editors. The poem's rhymes are mostly feminine, as was the case with Polish models (stress in Polish is always penultimate). One of St Dimitri's rhymes in this poem is dactylic, however, though this innovation vis-à-vis the Polish models was not unusual among early East Slavic poets. See M. L. Gasparov, *A History of European Versification*, trans. G.S. Smith and Marina Tarlinskaja (Oxford: Clarendon Press, 1996), 220–31.

[2]This poem seems to rely on an identification of Mary Magdalene (Lk 8.2, Mk 16.9, Jn 20.1–2, 11–18, and the other Gospels' resurrection accounts) with the harlot who anointed Jesus' feet (Lk 7.36–50). This conflation is fairly common in Latin tradition but rare, if not unknown, in the Orthodox liturgical and patristic tradition.

And have received remission of your sins.
I still desire to fall at his feet,
And, as a sinner, lament more, over much.
Step away, Magdalene, who have loved Christ without deceit,
And pressed yourself close to his holy feet.
You have already sweetened your heart to surfeit,
You have pleased him with a loving kiss.
I wish to press myself close to my beloved God
And fervently kiss his pure feet.

The Answer of Magdalene to a Sinner
Our Lord is compassionate to all, contains all spaciously,
Receives all, is glad for all, loves all, as is well known.
If all the people from all the world were to come,
There would be room[3] for all of them at the feet of my Christ.
And so together with me cling to his feet,
And, as I concerning mine, concerning your own sins do you
    pray.

[3]Literally, "It would be spacious."

14

Psalms, or, Spiritual Cantos[1]

Psalm 1

My Jesus most beloved,[2]
Sweetness of heart,
Only comfort in sorrows,
My joy,

Say to my soul: "For you am
I salvation,
The cleansing of sins
And entrance into paradise."

For me to you, O God, it is good
To cleave,
And on your loving-kindness
To hope.

No one can help me,
A sinner, in my afflictions,

---

[1]These eight poems are composed in a variety of meters: the first alternates eight-syllable lines with five-syllable lines (a slight variation on the 7+6 thirteen-syllable lines employed elsewhere by St Dimitri and discussed above, p. 117, footnote 1), and the second alternates five- and six-syllable lines (a sort of visual variant of Polish and then East Slavic hendecasyllabic verse; see Gasparov, *History*, 228). Various rhyme schemes are also employed for each. Though there is generally no regular rhythm, nevertheless rhythm is sometimes used to great effect. For example, in the first stanza of the third poem, "You are my God, Jesus," the last three lines of that stanza ("You, my gladness / You, my joy, / You, my sweetness!") can all be read as pairs of dactyls, with the prosodic stress falling, in each case, on the word "you" and then on the stressed syllable of the word "gladness," "joy," or "sweetness."

[2]In the original, there is an acrostic: "Hieromonk Dimitri."

If not you, O all-good
Jesus, God!

My only desire
Is to be with you:
Grant me always to hold
You, Christ, in my heart.

Will to dwell in me,
Reveal your good to me;
Me, sinful, unworthy,
Do not disdain.

Life has disappeared in pain
Apart from you, God:
You are might and health to me,
You are great glory.

I rejoice in you
And exult,
And you unto all ages,
God, do I praise.

Psalm 2

My hope
I place in God.
To his providence
I give myself over wholly.

Just as he wishes,
So shall he arrange [matters] concerning me,
But his will
Shall no one rearrange.

The judgments of God,
These are a great abyss.[3]

[3]Ps 36.7.

In secret counsels
Who shall attain to God?[4]

If something to someone
He should desire to give,
People's envy
Cannot oppose this.

If something is set
For someone by him,
Then without delay
It shall be fulfilled.

Therefore may my
Hope be for God—
Upon me he shall make marvellous
His great mercy.

I do not hope
On princes and people.[5]
The one who hopes in these
Is everywhere put to shame.

You are my portion—
You, the one God.
Your right hand
Helps me in all things.

Your right hand—
It creates strength,[6]
It heals the soul,
It gives health to the body.

These and all good things,
If they are needed,

[4] Cf. e.g. Ps 138.6.
[5] Cf. Ps 145.3.
[6] Cf. Ps 117.16.

It can quickly grant—
And afterwards, [it can grant a person] to live in heaven.

Psalm 3

You are my God, Jesus,
You, my joy,
You, my gladness,
You, my sweetness!

If I were to lose
All my things in the world,
You, all the more, my God,
Would I always have in faith.

Earthly riches
I consider nothing
When, gazing upon heaven,
I know you, the God of all.

If you afflict me,
I ought to stay steady.
If you strike me,
I will praise you.

I love you, my God,
Most holy over all,
I praise you, my King,
Most worthy of all.

Break down the stony
Door of my heart,
Place in us love
Flaming for you.

If people
Were to know you, O Christ,

You would they never
Anger by their sins.

If we should come to know you
In cherubic supplication,
Then we shall glorify you
In seraphic praise.

All-fervently we desire
To know you, O Christ.
Make us worthy to behold
You face to face.[7]

Psalm 4

I bring praise
To sweet Jesus,
For he is my glory
And the praise of all,
Jesus most beautiful![8]

Glorified in Trinity,
Unattainable for all,
Creator of the archangels,
Fighter against demons,
Jesus most beautiful!

Joy of monks,
Sweetness of priests,[9]
Grant joy even to me,
The sweetness of salvation,
Jesus most beautiful!

[7]Cf. 1 Cor 13.12.

[8]*Prekrasnyj* may mean, literally, "most beautiful," or, in a more modern idiom, "wonderful."

[9]These two phrases derive from the first ikos of the *Akathist to Our Sweetest Lord Jesus Christ*.

Do not drive me away,
Holy One, seek me out
Who lie in sins
And who do not rise,
Jesus most beautiful!

Creator of those on high,
Redeemer of the earthly,
Do not forget me,
Do not destroy me,
Jesus most beautiful!

O! King most glorious,
Immaculate lamb,
Hope in death,
Life of all after death,
Jesus most beautiful!

Garment of the beautiful
Heavenly Father,
Garb me with this
Caress[10] of yours,
Jesus most beautiful!

Joy of those who sorrow,
Staff of the aged,
Grant me comfort
[And] success in struggles,
Jesus most beautiful!

Do not abandon me,
Creator, seek me out,
Shepherd all-compassionate,
Most loving-kind,
Jesus most beautiful!

[10]Or, kindness.

Not according to my deeds
But according to your compassions
Judge me, Lord,[11]
Hetman[12] of the powers on high,
Jesus most beautiful!

Receive this
My small supplication
And quickly hasten
To be tender toward me,
Jesus most beautiful!

A final supplication
I bring to you
And with humble heart
I cry out unto you:
Jesus most beautiful!

Psalm 5

Christ my God,
Sweetest Jesus,
My Savior
Very most magnified!

Grant me ever
To live in your will,
And your Passion
To bear in my heart.

Seeing your image, may I
Know the holy God,

[11]*Pane*, the vocative form of *pan*. This is the Polish word for "Lord" (Slavonic *Gospod'*), used in Ruthenian to mean "mister" (Russian *gospodin*, Polish *pan*), but clearly meant in the former sense here.

[12]*Getman*. A term for a Cossack leader of the highest degree. St Dimitri was himself from a Cossack family; his father, Sabbas Grigor'evich Savich, was a Cossack *sotnik* ("centurion" or "colonel").

And into your hands
Commend my spirit.

Just as you wish
Do with me, God,
May the darkness
Of sin not cover me with gloom.

Lord God,
Your deeds are marvellous.
Receive the tender words
Of your servants

Which are prayers
They bring to you;
And your Mother
They honor with songs.

Psalm 6

I have far exceeded measure,
O my eternal God,
In my daily evil deeds.
Who shall help me in this?

I have transgressed the law,
O my mighty God,
And who now shall
Help me, a sinner,

Unless you, Father,
High in mercy,
Give me a hand
In my lowly state.

For all my
Years I have wasted prodigally;

In worldly vanities,
I, a sinner, have abode heinously.

On this account shall I take on
The appearance of the prodigal son,[13]
I shall go, I shall pray
To the heavenly Father:

I have sinned, Father,[14]
And the guilt is mine,
I am not worthy to be
As a son to you.

I have sinned against you,
Loving-kind[15] Father.
Be merciful to me,
Pray I, the malicious one.[16]

But these sins, which I
Have committed from my youth,
Remit, forgive,
According to your goodness.

And teach me
To live immaculately,
Henceforth keep me
From the net of sin.

So today shall I be
Your hired worker,[17]
Your true servant,
True novice.[18]

[13] Cf. Lk 15.11–32.
[14] Cf. Lk 15.18, 21.
[15] *Miloserdnyj.*
[16] *Zloserdnyj.*
[17] Cf. Lk 15.19.
[18] Or, "one true in obedience." The usual Slavonic term for a monastic novice, *poslushnik*, means "one under or in obedience (*poslushanie*)."

Grant me to live
Always according to your will,
[And] after life here
Heaven to receive.

Psalm 7

I cry out to God in my distress[19]—
May he hear me
And in my great sorrow
Comfort me with gladness.

He shall attend and transform
My lamentation into gladness and into joy,[20]
And lead my heavy burden of evil
Unto good.

I know not whence the wind shall blow up
In sweet coolness,
Yet I fall away from everything
In freedom.

Hope makes me firm,
A thought guides me,
It commands me to go toward God,
Who arranges everything.

If I were hidden under the earth,
Even there would he direct me.
If I were enclosed in stone,
Even there would he trouble me.[21]

[19]Cf. Ps 119.5 and 17.6 (and also 2 Sam 22.7).
[20]Cf. perhaps Ps 29:12, Esth 9:22.
[21]This and the preceding image clearly point to the grave and to the tomb, and echo the words of Ps 138.7–10.

But I stand far away,
And after the example of the sinner,[22]
I say: O! Why have you
Abandoned me, the passionate one!

Make ripe the time for the correction
Of my life,
For from my infant years
I have done much evil in this life.

Have mercy on me, a sinner,
O my eternal God!
And in your holy ears
Receive yet my cry.

Also grant me the endurance
Of all my sufferings;
Guide me, just as you know,
By your Holy Spirit.

If you will to punish [me],
Your will be done,
Only may my soul
Mercifully be saved.

All day, all night I shout aloud,
My Lord, unto you:
Hear my prayer
And take it unto yourself.

So grant me your mercy,
Deliver me from torment,
Inasmuch as I have totally fallen,
Through sin, right into your hands.[23]

[22]Cf. Lk 18.13.
[23]Cf. Heb 10.31.

Psalm 8

Loving-kind Mother!
You are a wall;
Against the evil, ferocious enemy
You protect me always.

He, the ferocious one, roars
[And] hunts me, the lowly one;[24]
Quickly, quickly your help
Delivers me from him.

At every hour I call,
I call out in infirmity
With a mighty cry, Mother; to you,
Pure Virgin, do I pray.

I do not know my end,
Its day [or] hour:
To you, to you, the Queen of all
Shall I direct my eyes.[25]

I ask you, all-compassionate,
Loving-kind Mother,
Hear my voice, hasten to my lamentation,
I pray you, all-compassionate.

May I raise up my hands
To your Son, O Mother;
O Mother most good,
Intercede before him.

To you, Virgin, do I pray,
I call out with a mighty cry,

[24]Cf. 1 Pet 5.8.
[25]Cf. Ps 24.15.

Bowing head,
Soul, [and] heart in groanings.[26]

[26]Cf. perhaps Rom 8.26; note also the earlier mention of the Theotokos' interces-
sion. The imperative there was *khodatajstvuj*; in Rom 8.26 the Spirit *khodatajstvujet*.
See also Prayer of Manasseh 11. (My thanks to Fr Ignatius Green for pointing out this
latter possible resonance.)

15

Verses on the Lord's Passion[1]

A very dread substitution, an unexpected substitution,
Ah! terrible to speech, to sight, and to hearing.
The King of heaven and all the earth, the Creator of the whole
    world,
By a most violent beast is betrayed to the violent,
By thrice-cursed Judas to the regiments of the Jews,
The most unmalicious lamb to wolves thirsty for blood.
He is exceedingly sorrowful in soul, seeing the cup of death,
He weeps bloody sweat, ah, because of our malice.
He who bears our sins falls to the earth,
Lifting eyes to heaven, he cries, "Father!"
But there is no [Father's] voice [saying,] "Behold, this is my
    beloved Son."[2]
For not to Tabor, but to Golgotha he is led.
There is no Peter saying, "It is good for us to be here,"[3]
Only Judas with troops, seeking to kill him.
He deceitfully kisses him in whose mouth no lie is found,[4]
In this way he betrays him to the beast-like Jews.
And they dragged him, bound with chains,
Along the way, and they gave him over to unrighteous judges.
They condemned him to death unrighteously,

---

[1]This poem is composed of thirteen-syllable (that is, 7+6) lines arranged in rhyming couplets. Isosyllabism and the caesura are quite strictly observed, though there are a few apparent exceptions to the former. See above, p. 117, footnote 1.

[2]Mt 17.5; Mk 9.7; Lk 9.35.

[3]Mt 17.4; Mk 9.5; Lk 9.33.

[4]1 Pet 2.22 (cf. Is 53.9).

And after many tortures they nailed him to the cross.
Behold, everyone, see the instruments of murder and torture:
The rope, the scourge, the pillar, the lance, the iron hands.
Behold, how evilly and dishonorably he suffered for us,
He who has crowned you with glory [and] honor.
Beholding these things, weep, sigh, feel pity,
Do not be like an inanimate rock.
Beholding the Creator dead, the rocks split,
The earth, full of terror, shook greatly,
All of creation was changed and seized by fear
Seeing the tortures on the cross and him taken down from
    upon the cross.
Fall down and kiss[5] the one laid in the tomb,
Kiss[6] with heart and mouth the one who died for you.
And come here, you young children,
Receive the cruel instruments one by one.
Taking them, let us go before the most pure body.

First Child
Behold, with humility, I fall down first
And tenderly receive the honorable ropes.

Second Child
With you I receive the soldier's hand
Which first began to create torture for the Creator.

Third Child
Command me to take the scourge and switch.

Fourth Child
With tenderness give me the pillar, I pray.

Fifth Child
Bowing down, I receive this crown of thorns
With which the new King of the Jews was crowned.

[5] *Lobyzaj.*
[6] *Tseluj.*

Sixth Child
That which was given to the abused God,
The reed, given as a scepter, I accept with fear.

Seventh Child
The nails by which the hands and feet of Jesus
Were pierced, four in number, I accept.

Eighth Child
The hammer that nailed Christ painfully to the cross
Accepting with kissing, lovingly I shall bear.

Ninth Child
I bow my humble head to the reed,
Sweetly I accept that which was filled with gall and vinegar.

Tenth Child
More precious than gold, more honorable than silver,
I bear the lance that punctured Christ's side.

Eleventh Child
I dare to bear after you others[7] the cruciform bed
On which you[8] lay, my Creator and God.

Ad Suos[9]
Taking these things, let us go before the most pure body.
Sending up glory, let us all cry out this song of burial:
"The noble Joseph," and so on.[10]

First Child
Attend, O every pious person,
To what the dishonorable council of Jews did.
The sons of night took Christ by night.

[7] Note the plural.
[8] And note especially the switch the singular (and change in addressee) here.
[9] Latin for "to one's own [company]."
[10] The incipit for a hymn used on Holy Saturday and the Sunday of the Myrrh-Bearers (Third Sunday of Pascha), and also said quietly by the priest or bishop at each divine liturgy.

Unmercifully with these ropes they bound [him.]
Woe! They bound the lamb, who is unmalicious,
Who went to the sacrifice for you, O man.
They made him [like] a chick in the heavens with a net of
    ropes,
They caught the firstborn of the most pure Virgin.
She wrapped him softly in swaddling clothes,
The soldier's hand bound him with a rope most firm.
The flower of Jesse is bound in the midst of the garden,
The ear[11] of most pure fruit of Mary is bound.[12]
O evil Judas, you lay a rope upon the Lord,
Soon you yourself shall become acquainted with a rope on
    your neck.
You said, "I do not receive glory from men,"[13]
Christ, [and] today dishonor has sought out your head.
You have the authority to bind, to loose,
Why did you give yourself over to be humiliated so?
Ah, the fierce soldiers drag you unmercifully,
The blessed seed falls along the way.[14]
He by whom Israel was led out of Egypt by night,
By night this one is betrayed into bonds by Israel.
O Jesus, violently bound by ropes today,
May I ever be bound to your love!

Second Child
Jesus stood before the high priest Annas,
Mercilessly greeted by this hand.
His holy face shines like the sun;
An iron hand darkens it with bruising
[And] loudly strikes the one who is meekly silent.

[11]That is, ear of grain (*klas*).
[12]*Vjazhestsja* is the word here and immediately above. This is the verb commonly used for binding sheaves of grain.
[13]Jn 5.41.
[14]Cf. Mk 4.4, Mt 13.4, Lk 8.5. Note that, in the parable, the seed fallen along the path (way) is trampled underfoot.

It tests whether or not he shall say, "Why do you strike me?"
Silent, God bore the wounds of his whole body,
For he was able to cover them with a garment.
It was not possible to cover his face most bright,
Which that hand, alas, wounded godlessly.
It has five fingers, it foreshadows the five great wounds,
[Which] it smoothly inscribes on the face ahead of time.
Christ is a good field—thus the Church proclaims—
[Which] the iron hand plows, [and] wounds with death.
The darkened people strikes the cornerstone[15]
With iron so that flame may shine on them.
Blinded by malice, not seeing the truth,
He sought it with his hands, of his own compulsion.
O sweetest Jesus, life of all life,
You gave over your cheek to all reproaches.
You did not forbid him to slap your face most bright;
Do not forbid us to behold your face in heaven.

Third Child
The hand plowed Christ's face mightily,
The scourge and the switch plow his whole holy body.
You plow, Jewish evil, but shall not reap,
But we henceforth shall taste the heavenly bread.[16]
You execute the benefactor, in whom there is no crime.
Out of your own stupidity, you [would] instruct eternal
    Wisdom.
Not by your power does he stand stripped naked,
But rather by the love of those who love him is he consumed.
Who gave this counsel to Jewish malice,
So that it made the coolness bitter to the one who is sweet?
Ah, so as to know not the most pure one beyond the wounds of
    his body,

[15]Cf. Ps 117.22.
[16]Or, grain.

They bind the switch, the scourge—alas!—to his flesh to the
    fullest.
From the top of the honorable head to the holy feet
No places have remained whole for Christ God.
Look with your mind, O man, on the Son of God,
How he stands up to his knees in his own pure blood.[17]
Say with tenderness: alas, God the Word,
On account of my sin your most precious blood has spilled out,
On account of me, an ingrate. Woe, alas, woe,
Your most pure blood is poured out like the Red Sea.
You who plunged Pharaoh's horns[18] into the sea[19]
Have drowned our many sins in your blood.
Lead us, pure one, into the promised land
Prepared for all in the heavenly habitations.

Fourth Child
Christ God, who is called a firm pillar,[20] the head of the
    Church,[21]
Is mercilessly bound to this pillar.
For the empty-handed [there comes] a blessing from the holy
    hands
Which are tied back [in preparation] for great torture.
Of old a pillar of cloud by day, of fire by night,[22]
Was their guide when they were led from the captivity
Of Israel; now [Israel] has captured God with a pillar
When he bound him to it. O what great malice!
He led them across dry land, and they have made

---

[17]An image of Christ treading the winepress; cf. Is 63.3. This was a common
motif in Western Christian art from the late Middle Ages right through the Reformation and Counter-Reformation. Cf. Gertrud Schiller, *The Iconography of Christian
Art*, trans. Janet Seligman, vol. 2 (Greenwich, CT: New York Graphic Society, 1972),
228–29.
[18]Ps 74.11.
[19]Cf. e.g. Ex 15.4.
[20]Cf. perhaps 1 Tim 3.15–16; cf. also 2 Tim 2.19, Eph 2.19–22.
[21]Cf. e.g. Col 1.18 and Eph 5.23.
[22]Cf. Ex 13.21 and elsewhere.

Their crossing in the blood of God, desiring to kill him.
Come, you[23] Judas, by whom the bread
Was soaked in the dish and eaten:[24] imbibe the blood of Christ.
Smite Christ the rock, no longer in the desert,
And for blood, not water. O mercilessness!
O, how, earth, shall you not collapse from under the pillar;
Seeing the Creator tormented, why do you not tremble?
The people, which of old heard a voice from God in the pillar,
Lest it [now] hear [God's voice], has closed his mouth with
     blood.
Solomon the king reigns on pillars of cedar,[25]
The King of heaven sorrows, tied to a [pillar] of stone.
O our sweet Jesus, wiser than Solomon,
O most beloved Jesus, much mightier than Sampson,[26]
Tear up this pillar, strike your enemies,
Let them perish, deprived of your mercy unto the age.

Fifth Child
When Jesus was released from the pillar,
He thought that he was free from the Passion.
But insofar as thorns penetrate deeply into his head,
Christ again cries out, "I have returned to the Passion!"
O, would someone have given my eyes a sea of tears,
I would have swiftly poured them out, seeing such pain.
Ah, the most holy eyes drown in blood,
The holy face and ears swell[27] with blood.
The one who grants kings golden diadems

---

[23]In Slavonic, the word is *semo*, "that," but using a demonstrative adjective with a proper noun in English is odd, and especially so when that proper noun is a vocative.

[24]Cf. Jn 13.26.

[25]Cf. 1 Kg 7.2–3.

[26]Cf. Judg 16.28–30.

[27]A play on words: the verb *zaplyvat'* refers primarily to swimming and, by extension, to swelling. The swimming image of course coordinates with the drowning image in the previous line.

Is crowned with a crown of thorns—ah, tormented.
There is the thorn of trees, [there] the head of kings, the divine
    throne.
God, the bloody rose, grows red among the thorns.
The crown encircles the most exceedingly holy head,
God suffers in the midst of the whole world, so that the world
    may know
That his head guides the circle of the world.
Who knows: do the thorns pierce it or the world?
Did not the earth sprout forth the thorns for the head?[28]
Being wholly his footstool, it is exalted in glory.[29]
Lest man wound with thorns
His feet while walking, God places them on his own head.
He who knows about the evangelical seed[30] shall confess
That Christ, the heavenly seed, has now fallen among thorns.[31]
"In affliction you shall be crowned with crowns,"[32] spoke
Isaiah; now we all behold this face-to-face.[33]
Joyfully you crown man with honor,[34]
You who, insulted, bear the royal title.
And the crown has roots in your head:
You remember about the glory given you by men.
Christ, insulted in a thorny diadem,
Grant us a heavenly crown with the saints!

Sixth Child
The king of kings, Christ our God, who reigns throughout the
    whole world,
Who gives crowns, sceptres, and purple robes to all kings,
Is now clothed in a stinking crimson robe

[28]Cf. Gen 3.18.
[29]Cf. Ps 98.5.
[30]Cf. Mt 13.7, Mk 4.7, Lk 8.7.
[31]Cf. Jn 12.24.
[32]My efforts to identify the source of this citation have failed.
[33]Cf. 1 Cor 13.12.
[34]Cf. Ps 8.6.

And, as an insult, receives a reed in his right hand.
The right hand glorified in might unto the ages[35]
Is now honored by a trembling reed.
Since we men are a wavering reed,[36]
So that we may be constant, God holds it in his right hand.
The Hebrew race makes an image of inconstancy,
Falling to their knees, saying,
"King of the Jews, rejoice,"[37] though they do not know the
    King;
Since they do not believe in righteousness, they confess him in
    malice.
Kings rejoice, ruling peacefully,
But you, our King, weep, you who are crowned tumultuously.[38]
You sprinkle your crimson robe with tears, as with pearls,
Which swim in the holy, weeping apple of your eye.
Why do you weep, when they say to you, "Rejoice"?
He weeps, because they spit together with their words,
Strike him on the ears, slap him on the cheek.
Our light has no appearance of comeliness.[39]
They who should tremble at heart wagged their heads,[40]
Not knowing that you are the King of kings,[41] the King of
    glory;[42]
They did not know, for you were not yet on the throne of the
    cross,
But rather in the stinking and dishonorable place of torture.
No one could have caught sight of this kingdom;
They shall behold it when you, having suffered, are glorified, O
    God.

[35]Cf. Ex 15.6.
[36]Cf. Mt 11.7.
[37]Cf. Mt 27.19, Mk 15.18, Jn 19.3. Consider also above, p. 45, footnote 1.
[38]Cf. Mt 27.29, Mk 15.17, Jn 19.2, 5.
[39]Cf. Is 53.2.
[40]Cf. Mt 27.39, Mk 15.29.
[41]Cf. 1 Tim 6.15; Rev 17.14, 19.16.
[42]Cf. 1 Cor 2.8.

Seventh Child

These are the nails, four in number,
By which the hands and feet of Christ were pierced.
These holy things dug into both hands and feet,
Adding unto torture [another] torture of great cruelty.
The one who opens his almighty hand,
Who feeds every living thing of his good will,[43]
His hands are hammered down—they held them fast with nails
In order to oppose the compassion of the compassionate God.
But this obstacle is no help to the malicious;
When the one who is nailed then grants paradise to the thief,[44]
To his Mother he commends John as a son.
"Woman, behold your son. Behold your mother," he says.[45]
The son of perdition[46] nails down the hands of the Creator
Lest he bring to pass the salvation of the world.
The zealous one works salvation for all in order to save [all],[47]
For the Creator does not desire the death of all sinners.[48]
He who is nailed by the hands causes the earth to tremble,[49]
Tears the curtain,[50] terrifies all creation.
He has the power to do all, he has the power to give all,
To clench [and] hold in his right hand wealth, glory, authority.
By the nails, like keys, the wounds [. . .][51]
Have found wealth not for themselves, but for us.
By this treasure I am redeemed from hell;
You who delivered me, God, be blessed!

[43]Ps 144.17.
[44]Cf. Lk 23.43.
[45]Cf. Jn 19.26–27.
[46]Cf. Jn 17.12.
[47]This word is supplied, for metrical reasons, by the editor, Bishop Amphilochius.
[48]Cf. Ezek 18.23, 33.11.
[49]Cf. Mt 27.51.
[50]Cf. Mt 27.51, Mk 15.38, Lk 23.45.
[51]A lucuna in the manuscript. Clearly, some word like "opened" should come next.

Eighth Child

By this hammer God was violently nailed to the cross,
The King of pain is seated on the throne of the cross
By the impious council of the filthy Pilate.
In him I saw no guilt; he condemned him to be crucified.
He who has condemned him to death should
Wash his hands and sacrilegious tongue, that he may see and
    say, "Why?"
For the sacrilegious tongue said, "I have the power to release,"[52]
But in thought he desired to nail him to the cross.
By the King of heaven he was commanded in a dream, he who
    did not command himself,[53]
For he trusted better an earthly Caesar.[54]
To these things, each man, may you attend,
You who consider the command to be a dream of yours.
[It is necessary] to make an inscription on your heart of stone[55]
    with this hammer,
[The hammer] with which the tormenters grind the
    cornerstone.[56]
The most precious diamond was tried by this hammer,
He was washed with his own lamb-blood, he who was broken.
The Mother's heart also broke
When she heard the sound of this hammer nailing.
So many blows, so many swords she had in her heart
When the murderers crucified him mercilessly.
Noetic paradise, our Jesus, bringing forth fruit unto the ages,
From four wounds you poured out four rivers for us.[57]
O man, you have an oar—an iron hammer;

[52]Cf. Jn 19.10
[53]Cf. Mt 27.19.
[54]Cf. Jn 19.12.
[55]Cf. Ezek 11.19 and 36.26.
[56]Cf. Ps 117.22.
[57]Cf. Gen 2.10 and also the fourth verse at the Beatutudes at the matins of Holy
Friday, the Service of the Twelve Passion Gospels.

You have four rivers to sail toward life eternal.
Have only [these] four [things] continually in mind:
Death, judgment, the flame of hell, and the kingdom prepared
    for the good.

Ninth Child
All sweetness, desire, Jesus beloved,
Through this reed were you given bitterness to drink.
You who gave sweet water to drink in the desert
Drink bitter gall and vinegar. O mercilessness,
In which the whole world inexorably abides!
Now Jesus comes to know the bitterness of the world,
Not only gall and vinegar, but also the deadly poison in it,
Which he tasted himself: the immortal God died.
Sea drunk with a flood of sweetness
From the richness of this house, in a cruel
Drink, in gall and vinegar, you dissolve the poison.
God bore the whole Passion, [and] you killed him with this.
Nailed to the cross, he did not say, "It is finished!"
Until he was given your poison to drink.
Know you not, O world, after what God thirsts?
That man may quench his thirst with tears.
O man, imitate the wise Magdalene,
Say now the words which she said before.
Ah! You say, "I thirst," but the drunkards give no water;
Only tears flow from your eyes; drink the streams of tears!

Tenth Child
The reed [. . .][58] [the lance][59] killed Christ,
The lance caused our eternal life to die;
A treasure more precious than gold or silver[60]
Jesus' side poured forth for us today.

[58]There is a lacuna in the manuscript.
[59]Supplied by the translator based on the gender of the verbal form.
[60]Cf. Ps 118.72; cf. also Ps 18.11.

So that man may know what God sows,
He desired that the soldier uncover it with a lance.
Not by a rod, but a lance is the rock smote:
Beloved Jesus poured forth a stream of life for us.
Contrary to nature, God has himself a writer;[61]
In the book of life he inscribes the letter[62] in a deadly manner.
It was beyond nature when the blinded soldier
Wrote[63] eternal life, and was enlightened.
The eye of his body and mind was blinded with evil,
Then he was clearly enlightened in both aspects.
Provoked to give Christ a bitter wound,
He was filled with sweetness, being enlightened.
O most sweet Jesus, you yourself taste bitterness,
And you do pour out for us indescribable sweetness.
Sweetness, but not sweetness for all—it is bitterness to
    unbelievers,
[But] more than honey and honeycomb[64] for us right-
    believers.
[Go on and] persecute; persecuted[65] in the world, when we
    languish with hunger,
By this lance we shall obtain sweet honey as food for ourselves.
Do not give us up, Jesus, to the hunger of not seeing you
And do not send us into fire, to eternal hell.
Let Gehenna be quenched by your blood, and by water;
Through blood give eternal freedom from it to the faithful!

Eleventh Child
All you passing by, behold the pain of Christ,
If you see his pain as pain.
Say mentally concerning the cruciform bed of Jesus:

[61]*Pisets*. This passage seems to depend on the multivalency of the verb *pisati*: it can mean both to write and to draw, and, as such, to depict, to describe.

[62]*Pismja*.

[63]*Napisa*. This is the aorist of *napisati*, the perfective form of *pisati*.

[64]Ps 18.11.

[65]2 Cor 4.9.

How did he lie on it: who could say?
By the nails, by the hammer he is placed, lest he be torn away.
Ah, to whom could this bed not seem dread?
A thorny plant in place of a pillow; hands [and] legs lay
On nails, so that our God might sleep to the utmost.
Ah, a bed no way soft; ah, a sharp bed:
Upon it you lay in pain, O God!
Ah, I had been driven from paradise on account of a crime
     [committed] by means of a tree.
You lead me back into paradise, you who are fixed to a tree!
I was stripped naked by the delusive counsel of the serpent;
You are naked, you who are clothed with light![66]
You who bound the deeps full of the elements of the world,[67]
Today your most holy cross is a haven from the waves of the
     world.
Until then you had no place to lay your head,
Here have you willed to lie down with the restless world.[68]
With gall they kill to death otherworldly Peace,[69]
From the deathly sleep they arouse him with a sharp lance.
O, who could declare the violent pains
That you, O God, endured on account of me, a sinner.
Seeing these things, let every man consider,
Lest he somehow add passion to the Passion:[70]
Do not bind God by chaining yourself to evil;
Do not slap him on the cheek by being greedy to hunt after
     what is another's;
Do not condemn him to lashes by being an unrighteous judge;
Do not tie him to a stone by becoming stony-hearted;

[66] Ps 103.2.

[67] Cf. e.g. Ps 32.7, Job 38.16.

[68] *Mirom bezmirnym.*

[69] *Mir bezmiren.* "World" and "peace" are homophones in Slavonic (and modern Russian). Though they were spelled differently in late Imperial standardized orthography ("old orthography"), this was not necessarily the case in earlier periods.

[70] That is, lest he somehow add more suffering to Christ's suffering in his Passion.

Do not pierce his head with thorns by becoming lifted up with
        pride;
Do not give a reed into his hand by being inconstant;
Do not call him King of the Jews by being full of lying,
And do not spit in his eyes with shameful words;
Do not abuse him, by hunting after what is another's with your
        hands;
By having[71] a shameless pupil in your eyes,
Do not lay on God a stinking crimson robe;
Do not crucify him on the cross by living according to your
        own will;
Do not give him gall to drink, by tasting sweetness[72] gladly;
Do not pierce him to the depths of the heart with a lance—
Be merciful of heart, not a violent tormentor.
Christ bore [these] wounds on account of all evil deeds.
O, who can declare the power of this pain to its full extent?
Before then the stars in the palace of heaven could be
        numbered,
Before [one could declare the power of such pain], the separate
        drops in the sea could be counted.[73]
In [this] life, none can tally
The passions and pains that God endured for us.
It suffices all to bear in mind the Passion and the cross
Upon which God willed to die for us all.
Upon the cross our salvation dies;
Let no one seek salvation apart from the cross.

---

[71]This word is supplied by the original editor for metrical reasons.
[72]Or, pleasure.
[73]These expressions certainly have a scriptural ring: cf. e.g. Gen 15.5, 22.17, 26.4;
Is 40.15; Prayer of Manasseh 9.

16

General Confession of Sins, Pronounced by a Penitent before a Priest

I confess to the Lord God Almighty, glorified and worshipped in Trinity, Father and Son and Holy Spirit, and to the most blessed Ever-Virgin Theotokos Mary, and to all the saints, and to you, honorable father, what I have done in all my sins, by thought, word, deed, and all my senses,[1] for I was conceived in sins, I was born in sins,[2] I was raised in sins, and I have dwelt in sins after baptism, even up to this very hour. I confess also that I have sinned in extreme manner by pride, vainglory, haughtiness with eyes and also with clothes and all my deeds, envy, hatred, desire for honors, and also by avarice, wrath, sorrow, laziness, stuffing the belly, sodomite lust, desecration, unrighteous cursing, adultery, theft, robbery, every type of fornication, most exceedingly shameful impurities, drunkenness, gluttony, lazy babbling, fleshly lust, impure kissing and touching even with my child-bearing members, the mental desire to murder; with respect to faith, hope, and love by always receiving the body and blood of the Lord unworthily; by violent exhortations and deception, ignorance, neglect, transgressing in gifts given and received, practice of usury, stewarding church property in an evil manner, insufficient giving of alms, hardness toward the poor, in [insufficiently] wel-

---

[1] This portion of text is very similar to the *Confiteor* as recited at the beginning of the Tridentine Mass, and is certainly derived from some form of that prayer, though maybe via intermediaries. My thanks to Fr Ignatius Green for noticing this and informing me.

[2] Cf. Ps 50.7.

coming and giving hospitality to the lowly, stinginess toward the orphans entrusted to me, not visiting the sick and those in prison in accordance with the evangelical commandment, not burying the dead, not clothing the poor, not feeding the hungry, and not giving drink to the thirsty; by not rendering due veneration, honor, and celebration to feast days, both those of the Lord and of those saints who have pleased him, and by not remaining pure and sober on them; by agreeing to [do] evil against the one in charge and not being helpful before him; by not comforting those who ask and even harming them; by blaspheming and cursing elders and superiors, not keeping trust with my friends and benefactors, not fulfilling my given obedience, looking with impure conscience on bestial and animal intercourse; proud entrance into the church of God, standing, sitting, lying down, and going out of it inappropriately; carefree conversations in it, lawless activities, defiled conversations with others; touching the sacred vessels and the holy service with impure heart and defiled hands, [and] by performing the prayers, psalmody, and calling upon God indifferently in the church of God; by most exceedingly evil intention, meditation, and depraved teaching, lying opinion, senseless judgment, evil concord and unrighteous counsel, defiled enjoyment and delight, in free, excessive, impure, and vexing words, in lying, in enticements, in various curses, in unceasing slanders, stirring up quarrels and dissensions and laughing at others, in carefree mockery, in debates, in deceit, in wickedness, in whispering, in vain and futile joy and in all evil; complaining, blasphemy, joking, causing laughter, oversleeping, evil talk, reproach, defiled speech, insults, hypocrisy, keeping vigil against God,[3] bodily lust, prodigal thoughts, impure delights, concord with the devil, breaking God's commandments, neglect in offering love both for God and neighbor, by lustful and impure sight, hearing, taste, touch, and smell. I have perished in all my thoughts, words, will, and deeds. Inasmuch as in these and other lawless acts, by all those things by which only human

---

[3]The reversing of daytime and nighttime activities in opposition to the God-established order.

infirmity can sin against its God and Creator in intention, word, deed, or pleasure, or enjoyment—in all this have I sinned—I consider myself guilty before the face of God more than all people, [and] I acknowledge and confess this and all my other numberless sins that I have committed, whether voluntary or involuntary, in knowledge or ignorance, myself with myself or through others, or by tempting my brother, and those which, on account of their multitude, I can neither know, nor remember, though what I have remembered, I have said—inasmuch as I repent, regret, and consider myself guilty before the Lord my God—for what has been said and not said, on account of not remembering the multitude of my sins, so do I humbly pray to the most holy and most blessed Virgin Theotokos and all the heavenly powers, and all the saints well-pleasing to God, and to you, honorable father priest, in [all of] whose presence I have confessed these [things], that on the day of judgment you all might be witnesses against the devil, the enemy and adversary of the human race, that I have confessed all of this, and that you may pray for me, a sinner, to the Lord my God. And I ask you, honorable father, as one who have the authority given you by Christ God to absolve those things which have been confessed, to forgive and remit sins, that you absolve me from all these my sins, which I have described before you, cleansing me, forgiving me all these things; and also grant me a penance[4] for all my transgressions, for I truly regret my transgression, [and] I have the will to repent and henceforth to keep myself from these [things] as much as is possible, with God's help.

Forgive me, father, absolve me, and pray for me, a sinner. Amen.

And after this you may read a prayer to Christ, crucified for our sake, in order to recall his saving sufferings, undertaken for the sake of our sins, reading which [prayer] a person[5] attains some tenderness, and, as if by some fetter, is held back from transgressions, with a view toward correction and succeeding in a life pleasing to God.

[4]*Epitimija.*
[5]Or, man.

17

Prayer of Daily Confession to God of a Person Laying Down a Beginning of Repentance

Finding a lonely place, and being alone by yourself, sit down, considering your life, and bring to mind all the sins committed by you from your youth, both those confessed and those unconfessed. Recalling them all, sigh from the depths of your heart, beat your breast, fall to your knees, raise up your mind from the earth to the throne of God, surrounded by cherubim and seraphim, there beholding, with mental eyes, God—seated on a high and exalted throne, watching over your portion and looking upon all your ways, and being attentive to whatever you do wish to say—[and] fall before his most loving-kind feet, and with fear begin to speak to him in this way:

Beginning of the Confession

God most good, spring of goodness, abyss of mercy, my Creator, Redeemer, and Savior! To you, who know those things that are hidden, secret, who try hearts and reins,[1] I confess my sins, and I bring my lawless acts before your all-seeing eye, in the hearing of your angels and archangels. I have sinned, my Lord and Maker (*in this and that way.*)

Here, say all your sins, in order, quietly with your lips, as if whispering into the ears of the Lord, saying with remorse and shame on your face,

[1]Cf. Ps 25.2.

153

with trembling of heart, and with tears: "By this and that I have sorrowed you, my Lord." *Finishing confessing your sins, say:*

Behold my wounds and scabs and pustulent sores, O merciful physician! Behold my heavy burdens, O my good Lord! Behold my shame and my nakedness, O long-suffering Judge! By these my deeds I have sorrowed, angered, and vexed your goodness; by them have I defiled your image, afflicted your Holy Spirit, and driven my guardian angel away from me; by them have I have trampled on your most precious blood, shed for my sake, and counted it as nothing; by them have I lost the beauty of my soul, stripped myself naked of your grace, and made myself a den of thieves, an abode of demons and passions; by them have I corrupted the Church, redeemed by your blood, making my whole body filthy, making all my members into members of fornication, defiling my soul with filthy, blasphemous, proud, soiled, prodigal intentions, consenting to this, and delighting in these things; by these things have I become a joy to demons, a lamentation to angels, and my soul has perished, so my way of life lies in a tomb of evil, sprinkled with the dust of impurity, moored by the stone of cruelty. Behold, Lord, my lawless deeds, which have gone up over my head, multiplied even more than the hairs of my head, and even more than the sands of the sea; confessing these things, I expose myself, condemn myself, declare myself guilty, and not only for these that I have recalled, but also those which I do not remember, and which I do not understand to be sins, but are, and which I do not know how to confess: all these things I lay before your most great loving-kindness, all-merciful and unmalicious God.

So after such, and after so many, shameful deeds of mine, after the great darkening and mindlessness of my mind, after such violent falls, and such senselessness, at last I have come to myself, and from the depths of my despair I have caught sight of and come to see your great loving-kindness, which cannot be overcome by the sins of men, for you do not wish the death of a sinner,[2] but rather mercifully await his conversion, and did shed your blood unstintingly for the sake of

[2] Cf. Ezek 18.23, 33.11. Quoted in the first Orthodox pre-communion prayer.

sinners alone, that you might call them to repentance. Understanding this, I, the wretch, I, the sinner, who have surpassed the whole world in sin, a second devil through my evil deeds, an imitator of Judas, an associate of the crucifiers, I, wretched and lawless, an innavigable sea of all filth, a bottomless sink of all uncleanness, I, defiled, a shameless doer of all evil things, I flee and fall down before you, all-merciful and all-compassionate, cry with repentance in the pain of my heart: I have sinned, Father, against heaven and before you, I have sinned and done lawlessly, I have become a transgressor of your commandments, I have sinned, as no one ever before, I am not worthy to be called your son;[3] I am not worthy to catch sight of and to see the height of heaven;[4] I am not worthy to open my mouth before thee; until now I have been your enemy. But I pray your goodness, and I bring supplication to your beneficence:[5] have mercy on me, God, according to your great mercy, and according to your many compassions purify my lawless deeds.[6] Have mercy, forgive and purify, for purification is from you. Lord, if you will, you can purify me. I know that you will all to be saved:[7] therefore save even me. Since you can [accomplish] whatsoever you wish, incline unto mercy, O Lord, remember your mercies and compassions that are from of old,[8] and forgive my iniquities; do not remember my evil deeds; do not enter into judgment with your servant;[9] do not grant unto me according to my deeds; do not expose me in your anger, neither punish me in your wrath.[10] Open to me the doors of your goodness, open to me the doors of repentance,[11] receive me in repentance, and call me to reason; stand me up, who am fallen,

[3] Lk 15.19, 21.
[4] Cf. Prayer of Manasseh v. 9.
[5] *Nezlobiju*. Literally, unmaliciousness.
[6] Ps 50.1.
[7] 1 Tim 2.4.
[8] Ps 24.6.
[9] Ps 142.2.
[10] Ps 6.2; 37.2.
[11] Cf. the hymn *Open to me the Doors of Repentance*, sung after the matins Gospel during the pre-lenten and lenten seasons.

seek me who am lost, convert me who am ruined, heal me who am wounded, raise me who am dead. Lord God of powers, convert me, reveal your face to me, and I shall be saved: shine your face on your servant.[12] How long, Lord, shall you forget me to the end? How long shall you turn your face away from me?[13] Turn your face away from my sin, but do not turn your face away from me, for I am afflicted:[14] hear me quickly. I know that I am not worthy of the loving-kindness and love for mankind, but rather worthy of all the torments that hell has in store: I am worthy of the unsleeping worm, the gnashing of teeth, the outer darkness, [and] the unquenchable fire prepared for the devil and his angels;[15] I am worthy of Tartarus, at which Satan himself trembles. However, so much is your greatness, and so great is your mercy, there is no sin that conquers your love for mankind. Therefore I do not despair, but rather hope in your inexhaustible goodness, poured out continually on all without measure, and your ineffable loving-kindness. I hope[16] on you, Lord, and I hope[17] that I will not be put to shame unto the ages. You are my hope, God, a hope that is not put to shame. Do not put me to shame, Lord, at your dread judgment, before the multitudes of the heavenly powers and all your saints. I heartily regret that I have angered you, my Creator; by my malicious acts I have sorrowed your eternal and limitless goodness. Him whom I should have loved, and whose[18] commandments I should have kept, as if hating him I have given myself over to innumerable sins. Him whom I should have desired fervently, about him have I thought very little, and toward him I have been careless. Him with whom I should have been sweetly sated, him have I exceedingly embittered and rejected. Him to whom I should have clung, from him have I torn myself. Him to whom alone I have should lived,

[12]Ps 30.17.
[13]Ps 12.2.
[14]Cf. Ps 68.18.
[15]Cf. Mt 25.41.
[16]*Nadejus'*.
[17]*Upovaju*.
[18]In the original: "your."

to him have I died, but I live to sins, delights, and passions.[19] Him whom I should have feared and honored, him have I despised and dishonored in the least of his brethren[20] and in me myself, defiling my whole self with deeds and words and intentions. Him whom I should have thanked and doxologized unceasingly, abiding before him, from him have I turned away, from him have I fled along dissolute paths, and I have been lazy in opening my mouth to the glory of his most holy name. O my desire, O my merciful God, may you not be angry at me, a sinner, unto the end; for now I painfully regret all of this, and I do not cease from this regret. O that I had never angered my Lord! O that I had sooner been numbered among the dead rather than vex my good Lord! Why was I born, why was I raised, why do I even live until now, that I sorrow you, my Master, so gravely? May my heart now be torn apart by pain, may my stoniness fall apart and be broken up by pity; may I melt, like wax,[21] from interior burning, for I have lost my God, I have fallen from his grace, I have angered his compassion, I have estranged his affection, I have deprived myself of his glory, I departed from his merciful visitation. On this account my eyes know watery outbursts day and night; inasmuch as I have not kept your law, inasmuch as I have transgressed much, I have sinned much before you; on this account my heart is in tumult, for neither does it tremble at torment, nor is it exhausted on account of falling away from heavenly good things, so much as it is exhausted because I have angered you, altogether good, altogether sweet, altogether lovely, altogether delightful: this alone shall I never cease to regret, from now and unto the ages. May my life disappear in pain, and my years in groanings; may my soul be exhausted in pain, and may my bones be troubled[22] because I have gravely sorrowed my God, my Creator, my Master, my Redeemer. And what shall I do? I know that you are good, my God; you are loving-kind, my Creator; you are merciful and compassionate, my Redeemer—so merciful, that you

[19]Cf. Rom 6.1–11, esp. 2, 10–11.
[20]Mt 25.40, 45.
[21]Cf. perhaps Ps 21.15.
[22]Cf. Ps 6.3.

did not spare even your own soul, but rather laid it down for us sinners; and you do unto us not according to our lawless deeds, neither do you give unto us according to our sins.[23]

This shall I do: I shall collapse at your most pure feet, I shall worship and fall down, and I shall lament before you, the Lord who created me. I am an abyss of sins; I plunge myself into the abyss of your mercy, my God, and I pray you, guide me toward true repentance and lead me, who am senseless and stony, into sense. You have accepted many penitent sinners: David,[24] Manasseh,[25] Josiah,[26] the publican,[27] the harlot,[28] the prodigal son,[29] the thief,[30] Peter,[31] Saul,[32] Photini,[33] Thais,[34] Pelagia,[35] Mary of Egypt;[36] do not reject even me, who have exceeded these in sins. For you have not come to call the righteous, but rather sinners to repentance;[37] therefore call even me, who am most sinful of all; even if I have done nothing good before you,[38] grant me according to your grace to lay down a good beginning, and

[23]Cf. Ps 102.10 (and also Ps 6.2).

[24]See 2 Sam 12.1–25.

[25]See 2 Chr 33.10–20 and the Prayer of Manasseh.

[26]See 2 Kg 22.

[27]See Lk 18.9–14.

[28]See Lk 7.36–50.

[29]See Lk 15.11–32.

[30]See Lk 23.29–43.

[31]See Jn 18.15–18, 25–27 and parallels, and also Jn 21, esp. vv. 15–19.

[32]Cf. Acts 9.1–19.

[33]A traditional name for the Samaritan woman of Jn 4.1–42.

[34]According to the version of her *Life* included by St Dimitri in the *Lives of the Saints* under October 8, and which he attributes to St Jerome, St Thais was a harlot led to repentance by Abba Paphnutius.

[35]A harlot and actress of Antioch, led to repentance by St Nonnus. Her *Life* was written down by James the Deacon of Heliopolis and was, like that St Thais, included by St Dimitri in the *Lives of the Saints* under October 8.

[36]A repentant harlot and desert saint, whose *Life* was recorded by St Sophronius of Jerusalem.

[37]Mt 9.13; Mk 2.17; Lk 5.32.

[38]A phrase derived from earlier prayers. Cf., e.g., the first morning prayer, attributed to St Macarius the Great, in contemporary Russian prayer books. For the history of these prayers in the Slavonic tradition, see M. A. Verkhovskaja, "Lichnoe molitvennoe pravilo v liturgicheskoj praktike Russkoj pravoslavnoj tserkvi [The Personal Prayer Rule in the Liturgical Practice of the Russian Orthodox Church],"

make me worthy, Lord, to love you, just as I once loved sin itself, and to work for you without laziness, just as I earlier worked for Satan the deceiver.[39] All the more shall I work for you, Lord my God, Jesus Christ, all the days of my life, if you grant me your grace as a help.

Truly I marvel at your great long-suffering, O all-merciful, for during that time in which I committed my lawless deeds, you did not bring me before your righteous judgment, nor did you expose me in your anger, nor did you execute me in your wrath,[40] nor did you smite me with lightning from the heights, nor did you command the yawning earth to bring me down to hell alive,[41] nor did you allow some pointless death to steal me away; and when I marvelled much at this, I came to know that your measureless loving-kindness awaits my repentance and the correction of my defiled life with mercy and long-suffering, leaving me without execution so that I may come to my senses, and come to know my lawless deeds, and cease from my evil undertaking. I have come to know this, and with repentance I have come unto you not of my own doing, but rather you have guided me and led me to you. And for what reason you have done this, and what has moved you to such mercy, and what need you have that you call me, I do not know. This only I know, that I am sinful and without defense, and your enemy until now, and still uncorrected; but inasmuch as you have called me and lead me before you, therefore enlighten my mind, open my lips,[42] teach me how to

---

Svet Khristov prosveshchaet vsekh: Al'manakh Svjato-Filaretovskogo pravoslavnogo instituta [The Light of Christ Illumines All: The Almanac of St Philaret Orthodox Insitute] 12 (2014): 103–26, especially 110. According to Verkhovskaja, the prayers now found in the Russian Church's morning and evening prayers had become widespread in Slavonic books such as the *Sledovannaja Psaltyr'* [Augmented Psalter] by the 16C and 17C. Hieromonk Dalmat Judin's informally published work on the prayer rule in early printed books, available at his Academia.edu page and elsewhere, such as Bogoslov.ru, came to my attention too late for me to consider it here.

[39] A phrase derived from earlier prayers. Cf. the eighth prayer in the contemporary morning prayer rule of the Russian Church.

[40] Cf. Ps 37.2.

[41] A phrase derived from earlier prayers. Cf. the eighth prayer in the contemporary evening prayer rule of the Russian Church.

[42] Cf. Ps 50.17.

speak before you, and cleanse my many lawless deeds and filthy acts, sprinkle me with the hyssop of your mercy, make me whiter than snow,[43] lest I stand before you filthy and defiled. It would be better for me to hide somewhere in the dark bowels of the earth than to stand ashamed before the greatness of your unapproachable glory, shamefully stripped naked in this way, all covered in filth, revolting, while all your cherubim and seraphim who stand before you look upon me. But there is no place that can hide me from your eyes, brighter even than the sun.[44]

At this I marvel and am stupefied: how are you not so revolted by such filthy defilements of mine, and [how is it that you] allow me to stand before you and to speak boldly, and, what is more, unashamedly? How are you not revolted to gaze upon the impurity of my heart and the filth of my soul? How shall it be that your attendants, suddenly taking up fiery weapons, do not reject me and drive me away from your face?[45] How shall it be that, repulsed by me, they do not drag me, bound, into the outer darkness?[46] But your beneficence[47] and extreme compassion do not desire that it be this way, for great, truly great, is your mercy; higher than the heavens, deeper than the abyss of hell, wider than all the earth and sea is your goodness, which desires not my perdition, but rather awaits my conversion, and rejoices over the repentance of a sinner.[48] Great is your mercy, Lord, when you suffer long with me, who have many times promised to repent, and have fallen into the same things, even the most evil; for many times have I promised repentance, and have affirmed this with oaths; however, I, the passionate one, lied; I repent trembling, but shall you not yet smite me, Lord? And still I do these same things every hour; but yet you are still loving-kind to me, not destroying me together with my lawless deeds.

[43]Cf. Ps 50.9.
[44]Cf. Sir 23.19.
[45]Cf. Gen 3.24.
[46]Cf. Mt 22.13.
[47]Or, more literally, "unmaliciousness," "lack of malevolence."
[48]Cf. Ps 35.6–7, 2 Pet 3.9.

Glory to your longer-suffering, glory to your loving-kindness, glory to your compassion,[49] glory to the multitude of your compassions,[50] glory to the great multitude of your goodness, glory to your merciful face, standing before which I now bring to you, my Lord, my will and my goal set in hope of your help. From now on, from this day, from this hour, from this point, according to my strength I shall correct my evil and wretched life, feel pain and regret until death over past sins, and by your help keep myself from that which comes dangerously nigh. You know, my Lord, how I hate my filthy deeds and my very self on their account, and I hate my life all-defiled, and moreover I do not wish, by these things, to vex you, my good God—only do you, Lord, give me help; for without your all-powerful help and grace I can in no way separate myself from my evil deeds and sinful way of life, and so cannot do one good deed, for without you I can do nothing.[51] I have the will to repent; if you, God, shall help me, you can purify me. Lord, help me, and I shall be saved.

I believe, Lord, in your compassion: help my unbelief.[52] I believe that you are near unto all who call upon you in truth.[53] Truly, truly, truly I desire with all my heart to turn to you, my God, in repentance. God, hearken to my help; Lord, make haste to help me.[54]

Then, rising from the ground, being firm in your hope in the Lord, and considering his great goodness and mercy, read Psalm 102, that your soul may be comforted: "Bless the Lord, my soul, and my inner parts his holy name . . ."[55] *and so on.*

If it is not possible to learn all these phrases by memory, then lay down in your mind all these things with these short articles: 1. I confess to my God all my sins. 2. I judge myself unworthy of his loving-kindness, but rather worthy of eternal torments. 3. However, I do not

[49]*Blagoutrobiju.*
[50]*Shchedrot.*
[51]Jn 15.5.
[52]Mk 9.24.
[53]Ps 144.18.
[54]Ps 69.1.
[55]Ps 102.1.

despair. 4. Humbly I beg forgiveness. 5. I lay down the goal of correcting my life. 6. I believe without a doubt that my sins are forgiven.

18

Untitled Prayer

The humble Dimitri, Metropolitan of Rostov and Yaroslavl, wrote this for the use of his own wretchedness.

I know that my ascent [is headed] toward descent, life [is headed] unto its cessation, youth [is headed] toward old age. Because I live, I shall die, and, after death, I know not where I will be found. I blossom forth in youth, I dry up in old age, I rot away after death. If I am mortal, why do I live as if I never had to die? If I will die, then why do evil and falling-into-sin not die within me? If I shall have to return to dust and worms, to stink and evil stench, then why do I not return to what is better? If I shall be diligently tried and shall hear a firm answer, then why do I not soak all my members with tears and tremble with my whole body? For I shall go to my grave with great sorrow and affliction of heart, and there I shall see how my nature is changed, how my wretched body stinks from corruption, eaten by worms, [and] my bones are returned into the dust. And I shall ask my grave, and inquire diligently, "Where is the good appearance of my countenance, where is the brightness of my eyes? Where is the eloquence of sweet speech? Where are deeds most glorious? Where is [that] most sweet and most cheerful conversation with my friends? Where is every vain adornment and enjoyment of this world?" But I hear from my grave, "Here, here in this grave is all your comeliness: dust and ash, worm and evil stench. Look, look," it says, "at your comeliness, look, and diligently attend, and kiss me, your grave, with a loving embrace, for you will be dwelling in me until judgment day, awaiting the righteous judgment." When I shall stand and appear before the judgment of my unhypocritical judge and God, what shall

I, the unhappy one, then say? To whom shall I flee? What shall I say for my vindication? Oh, oh! Woe, woe! Alas, alas! For if there even the righteous is scarcely saved,[1] then I, very sinful, altogether most defiled, like a stinking dog—how shall I appear, having no wedding garment? But I, roused to attention, shall finish reading, wash my face with tears, and altogether fervently I shall entreat the most merciful God, my Creator: grant me, who am the very most sinful, the altogether most defiled, like a stinking dog, forgiveness of my sins, and, according to your ineffable goodness, to receive eternal life after my end; to be joyfully raised with body and soul together; to be counted worthy of standing at your right hand; [and] to praise you unto the ages without interruption, in accordance with the prayers of my indubitable hope, our most holy Lady, the Theotokos and Ever-Virgin Mary, and all your saints. Amen.

O man! Attend,
And never forget the hour of death.
Even if someone does not remember death,
Torment does not pass from him.

[1] 1 Pet 4.18 (Is 53.9).

APPENDIX I

Letter 22 to Theologus

[5 April 1708,[1]
Rostov.]
Christ is risen![2]

Beloved father Theologus, I greet you with the resurrection of Christ, with a white-red[3] egg, Christ himself, concerning whom a certain God-loving individual says in the Song of Songs, "My beloved is white and red":[4] white with purity, red with blood poured out on our behalf.

Be well,[5] beloved brother Theologus, and rejoice in the white-red egg, Christ, with respect to whom may your conscience be white, and your soul red. I myself desire for your honor an advantageous and lengthy abode in this white light,[6] [and] an eternal palatial dwelling among the beauties[7] of paradise. Amen.

[1]Pascha fell on April 4, 1708. The letter was therefore written on Bright Monday. The letter is translated from the text edited by M. A. Fedotova. See Fedotova, *Epistoljarnoe nasledie* [Epistolary Legacy], 95–96. The reader interested in the particular persons and works mentioned in the letter is directed to Fedotova's commentary, ibid., 284–85, which I saw, for the most part, no reason to reproduce here.

[2]Here, and throughout the letter, St Dimitri uses the more colloquial form *voskres* for Church Slavonic *voskrese*.

[3]Or, "light red"—that is, a pink or vermilion color. Eggs, dyed red, are commonly exchanged as part of the greeting rite of Paschaltide.

[4]Song 5.10.

[5]*Zdrastvuj.* This might also be translated, simply, "hello," or "greetings," but since it is linked here with another imperative ("rejoice"), the more literal translation was the better option.

[6]Or, "in this bright world," that is, in this present life.

[7]*Krasotax. Krasnyj* means both "red" and "beautiful," a double meaning that here allows St Dimitri to connect the redness of the Easter egg with the beauties of paradise.

Hasn't my chronicle-work piled up on you by now? Maybe it's time you send it to us? It's in vain that you've commanded me to copy it out—it can't be [done], since right now it's in different places,[8] inasmuch as other [parts],[9] are, with God's help,[10] being corrected, others shall be set aside, others shall be added, and some have already been corrected, and some added. A building isn't built all at once, nor is a book composed all at once, and after it is completed, the master looks over his work, correcting and verifying. I ask your holy prayers to help this work that I have begun. The soul is joyful in paradise, but sins won't allow it [to enter]. It is a joy to write, [but] my health is poor. It is little possible to labor, [but] very possible to be lazy. The hand trembles to write, but it does not tremble to taste beer [or] mead.

Please, beloved, I pray, find me St Andrew of Caesarea's commentary on the Apocalypse and buy it with your money. And what you pay, I ask you to let me know, and I will immediately send the money to your honor. For even if I have a commentary in Latin, twice over, in which St Andrew is cited,[11] nonetheless I want to have this Andrew himself, printed in the Slavonic language.

I wrote to Fr Archimandrite at the Monastery of the Caves, and spoke in person to the elder of the Caves, advising that they themselves reprint this[12] commentary on the Apocalypse, but I don't know whether they will have listened to my advice. And if they do listen, don't buy it and lose money; they will give it to me for free.[13] There will be news from Fr Archimandrite, who wants to come to Moscow for the archpriestly[14] consecration, concerning whose

[8] *Po inomu.*

[9] *Inaja.*

[10] Literally, "God hastening."

[11] Literally, "is recalled."

[12] Fedotova's edition has *tvoe,* "yours," here, but this would seem to make little sense; I therefore translate *toe,* "this."

[13] Literally, "without [my] buying [it]."

[14] *Arkhierejskoe.* This is a reference to an episcopal consecration. This use of *arkhierej* as a formal liturgical title for the bishop is not to be confused with the honorific title *protoierej,* often rendered in English as "archpriest," bestowed upon

arrival in Moscow, when it happens, let me know. But if they do not reprint this commentary, then ask I you to try to find it in Moscow [and] buy it,[15] I pray and bow to you.[16]

Humble Dimitri, Archpriest[17] of Rostov
5 April
P.S. To the most honorable Mr Fr Joseph, judge: Christ is risen!
To the most honorable Fr Karion: Christ is risen!
To the most honorable Mr Stephen Vasilevich: Christ is risen!
To the most honorable Fr Theologus.

certain senior presbyters.
[15]St Dimitri did eventually obtain a 1625 Kiev printing of the commentary; see Fedotova, *Epistoljarnoe nasledie* [Epistolary Legacy], 285.
[16]Literally, "beat my forehead." See above, p. 20, footnote 15.
[17]Or, "high priest." This refers to the episcopal rank. See above, p. 166, footnote 14.

A Psalm in Honor of St Dimitri

Make festival today, country of Russia,
Grace is given to us from the heavens.
Be glad today, city of Rostov:
Behold, the holy hierarch of Christ, Dimitri,
    The reverend pastor of the flock,
        Is revealed to us from the bowels of the earth.
Beneficent streams have poured forth for all.
Each [of you], approach in haste with faith:
You shall receive help, health, healing;
Only pour out fervent supplication.
    God rouses him to the voice
    Which asks that he fulfill all.
His virtue and faith
Are exalted in the presence of the Most High,
The city on top of the mountain has not been hid,[1]
But rather God has revealed it openly to all,
    Making strong the faithful in faith,
    And putting opposition completely to shame.
Be radiant, all [you] his flock, seeing
Such an archpastor;
Be put to shame, each opponent;
See, with darkness shaken from your eyes;
    Behold, the teacher of right faith,
    The uprooter of error.
Therefore, exult, Orthodoxy,
Glorifying the Creator because of these things.

[1]Cf. Mt 5.14.

God, look down, see your vineyard,[2]
Grant no thorn to grow up therein.[3]
    Such vinedressers even now
    Do you grant to your holy place.
So you, now with an incorruptible crown
Crowned, standing before the Creator,
Do not depart from us in spirit,
But remain and rouse our voice.
    From calumny deliver us,
    Guide each of our paths to good.

[2]Cf. Ps 79.15–6.
[3]Cf. Gen 3.18; Prov 24.31; Mt 13.7 (and parallels). The image of thorns growing up as a result of God's punishment or abandonment is common throughout the law and the prophets; many more verses could be cited here.